Ethel Brilliana Tweedie

Danish Versus English Butter Making

Ethel Brilliana Tweedie

Danish Versus English Butter Making

ISBN/EAN: 9783743435650

Printed in Europe, USA, Canada, Australia, Japan

Cover: Foto ©ninafisch / pixelio.de

More available books at **www.hansebooks.com**

DANISH

versus

ENGLISH BUTTER MAKING.

BY

MRS. ALEC TWEEDIE (*née* HARLEY).

AUTHOR OF "A WINTER JAUNT TO NORWAY," "A GIRL'S RIDE IN ICELAND,"
AND "WILTON, Q.C."

LONDON:
HORACE COX,
WINDSOR HOUSE, BREAM'S BUILDINGS. E.C.
1895.

"A WINTER JAUNT TO NORWAY."

CONTAINING

PERSONAL ACCOUNTS OF NANSEN, IBSEN, BJÖRNSEN, BRANDES, &c.

By MRS. ALEC TWEEDIE.

TWENTY-SIX ILLUSTRATIONS.

Second and Cheaper Edition, 7s. 6d.

Spectator (four columns of review): "The pages from start to finish are really a treat."

Times: "Breezy and entertaining."

Queen: "A most interestingly written account of a most adventurous journey."

Daily Telegraph: "Will well repay perusal."

Pall Mall Gazette: "Courageous sketching from nature."

Field: "Pleasantly written book; lively and entertaining style."

London: BLISS, SANDS, and FOSTER.

WILTON, Q.C.; or, Life in a Highland Shooting Box.

Second Edition. Price 6s.

Morning Post: "Mrs. Alec Tweedie now turns to fiction, which she treats in the same lively manner. There are many varied types among her characters, while touches of sentiment mark the scenes played by Lorna and her two admirers."

The Queen: "'Wilton, Q.C.' will be read and re-read for its excellent sketches of Highland customs and Highland sport. There have been few better descriptions of that life."

Dundee Advertiser: "The characters are portrayed with vigour, and the story is brightly written."

Scotsman: "Mrs. Alec Tweedie has much to tell that is at once racy and interesting, and those who love the Highlands will read her admirable word pictures with great pleasure. The story is eminently readable."

Glasgow Herald: "Has succeeded in bringing very vividly before the reader life in a shooting box. The sensational ending contrasts with the other parts of the book."

Sun: "Contains some very excellent sketches of life and sport. The story is well told."

Golf: "A racy and readable story."

London: HORACE COX, Windsor House, Bream's Buildings, E.C.

PREFACE.

An article entitled "Danish Butter Making" appeared in the *Fortnightly Review* for May. It met with much kindness from the press both in leading articles and columns of review, and brought besides numbers of letters from various parts of the country asking whether it would be reproduced in a different form.

Owing to the courtesy of Messrs. Chapman and Hall, and Mr. W. L. Courtney, the editor of the *Fortnightly Review*, I was allowed to use my paper as a pamphlet, in which guise it now appears with many additions. While formerly only dealing with butter making in Denmark, it now contains some information about English dairying, for which material I am indebted to the persons whose names appear within these pages.

If I have done anything to rouse our farmers from their lethargy I shall indeed rejoice. If I have failed I can only excuse myself by owning I am not a butter maker, as some papers seem to suppose!

E. B. T.

London, *July*, 1895.

DANISH *versus* ENGLISH BUTTER MAKING

CHAPTER I.

ENGLAND imported £13,470,419 worth of butter in 1894. That is to say, 2,576,063 cwt. of butter came into the country from foreign and colonial sources. Therefore, nearly *thirty-seven thousand pounds sterling* was paid out of the country every day for butter consumed by people unable to make it for themselves. These figures are somewhat startling.

About a third of the butter import came from Denmark. Thus it will be seen that Danish butter plays a very important part in the household economy of our British wives. Even our navy is largely provisioned with Danish butter! Sir U. Kay-Shuttleworth, late Secretary of the Admiralty, informed the House of Commons that the butter for the navy "was ordered from abroad, because our agriculturalists could not hold their own with Danish butter!" If "our agriculturalists" cannot compete with the foreigner, at least they might imitate him.

The yearly increase in our import of Danish butter is very great, and its excellence is widely acknowledged. Therefore a few words about its origin and manufacture may be of some interest.

It is only within the last twenty years that Denmark has made butter for export at all, and now butter-making is the chief trade of the country and the source of the greater part of its revenue. Denmark learnt dairying from the Holsteiners, and through them to some extent from the Dutch, but having once mastered their trade, the Danes were quick in grasping every opportunity of securing the best market. Industrious and painstaking in their work, not content with the extent of land under cultivation, between 1860 and 1881 they wrested for their own uses—

From the sea, by embankment 58,000 tönder land.
Tracts of land reclaimed by
    nature . . . . 3,000 ,,
By the drainage of fresh-water
    lakes, &c. . . . 20,000 ,,

Since the latter period they have been even more industrious in adding to their pasture lands!

The great importance of the dairy industry was recognised about twenty years ago by the Royal Danish Agricultural Society, who did everything in their power to help the farmers and encourage trade.

The Danish farmers also saw the advisability of combining and working together, and fully realised the advantage of employing modern scientific principles. They have also found that the quality of butter cannot be maintained where each farmer makes it according to his own method and after his own ideas; therefore individual butter making has practically been given up.

Farmers keep the cows and deliver the milk, or more often merely the cream—properly separated by centrifugal machines—to the butter-making factories, of which there are some hundreds established over the country. There, the butter being made on the newest scientific and hygienic principles, a certain standard of excellence is maintained. The result of this combination of labour, with improved methods of manufacture, is that the Danish farmer to-day is a rich man, with a regular business, instead of being discontented and impecunious, as so many of our own farmers are in England.

Here they tell us they cannot grow corn with sufficient profit to enable them to compete in the market with foreign grain, and they further add that they cannot rear beef and mutton at a price which would enable them to hold their own against foreign supplies. Granting, for present purposes, that this is perfectly true, does it necessarily follow that all other doors of profitable enterprise are closed against them? Are other nations to grow rich on our gold, by supplying us with necessaries which we cannot, or rather will not, produce for ourselves? Is our land to lie idle, and our country labourer to starve, or rush to swell the ever increasing population of the towns?

Surely if a little country like Denmark can find employment for her people, aye, and grow rich beside, on butter-making, we may take a lesson from her, and see whether something cannot be done to alleviate the misery of pastoral England. Naturally, expeditions starting for the North Pole have all their food supplies thoroughly analysed before deciding definitely which are the most suitable. Dr. Fridtjof Nansen took only Danish butter, much compressed, with him on his four or five years' experimental drift through Polar ice, and Mr. Frederick Jackson, who started from our shores last summer, is similarly equipped, for although, as far as possible, he chose everything English, he found our butter could not stand the severe tests so well as Danish. Danish and colonial butter are creeping in everywhere. Even in remote Sutherlandshire the native butter is so bad that Danish is chiefly used! Yet the Danish has to travel hundreds of miles, at no little expense, whilst the other, though made at the very door, is so badly churned that foreign produce takes precedence.

In the *National Review* for March, Mr. Inglis Palgrave, writing on agricultural depression, estimates the annual loss to farmers during the last fifteen or twenty years to be £25,000,000, while £2,800,000 less is distributed annually in wages. But yet we go on increasing our foreign imports of butter, bacon, and eggs, instead of trying to repair this disaster. Will no influential person take up this great question, sift the matter to the root, and sug-

Butter Making. 5

gest a remedy, or else induce England to follow Denmark's excellent example.

Without going further, the following table will give some idea of what England imports yearly from Denmark alone:

DENMARK EXPORTED TO ENGLAND.

	1889.	1890.	1891.	1892.	1893.	1894.
BACON:						
Cwt.	589,387	470,047	583,408	671,882	711,854	766,828
Value £	1,670,369	1,346,325	1,590,349	1,919,397	2,148,135	2,189,690
BUTTER:						
Cwt.	677,398	824,749	876,211	863,522	934,787	1,102,493
Value £	3,742,869	4,422,257	4,865,842	4,848,735	5,279,175	5,843,954
EGGS:						
Great hundred (120)	946,714	1,145,258	1,161,174	1,247,968	1,098,013	1,254,914
Value £	286,917	359,759	395,963	413,469	376,793	422,790

It is erroneous to imagine that Danish butter-making is a "State" business. Government exercises no control over the dairies and does not support the dairy schools. The State has nothing whatever to do with the matter, beyond arranging competitions and awarding prizes for excellence. These competitions are usually arranged at twelve hours' notice, so as to oblige the competitors to send in any butter they happen to have ready, instead of an extra good pound or two made with great care specially for exhibition.

The State, however, has gone so far as to provide a suitable building in which to hold these shows, where an even temperature can be maintained winter and summer, and these shows have done so much towards perfecting the manufacture of butter that we give the lines on which they are held :—

   * 1. A continuous butter show will be held at the expense of the State during several months of each year, and a suitable building will be provided, where an even temperature can be maintained winter and summer.

   2. Fresh samples of butter will be accepted every fourteen days, to remain on exhibition until the judges have given their decisions; firstly, on the sample as received, and, secondly, fourteen days later. The casks of butter will be submitted to the judges in no particular order, and so arranged that it will be impossible for them to be guided in their decisions by any outward sign or mark.

A visit made to the exhibition showed that every cask, on receipt, was weighed, first in bulk, and then the contents separately. The hoops at one end having been removed, the cask, with contents replaced, is lifted on to a funnel-shaped stand made of tin, in the bottom of which is a locked receptacle, containing a glass bottle, to receive the brine or water which percolates through the loosened staves. When the judges go their rounds the cask itself is further entirely concealed from view in a tin cover secured by lock and key to the stand above mentioned. An aperture at the top allows the contents to be tested.

In shows held previous to 1888, it had been found that many samples of butter classified as "finest" did not, after the lapse of a short time, merit that character. In order to obviate this objection there were in the future two distinct testings, with an interval of two weeks.

---

   * Report on Butter Show System in Denmark, No. 151.

"The loss of weight frequently complained of, and which sometimes takes place during transport from the dairy to the merchant's warehouse, may arise," says Professor Fjord, "from the water that comes from the butter milk being imperfectly pressed out. This fluid, mixing with the salt, runs off in the form of brine, and constitutes a fault in manufacture which ought not to occur." He goes on to remark, "It will now be an easy matter to determine the loss of weight during the fortnight that the casks remain on exhibition, and every facility will be afforded for ascertaining the cause of these defects.

"Dairymen desiring to take part in the shows must, as soon as they receive a communication by letter or telegram, at once (*i.e.*, on the same day) send in a ready-made cask of butter, and undertake to repeat this as often as required. Butter sent in for exhibition must not be pressed or kneaded again after receipt of such notice. The dairyman in this way will be unable, as in previous shows, to make one special cask of butter with an exhibition in view. It is the dairy's ordinary produce which is to be submitted.

"Competing dairies have, moreover, to send in a return of feeding and system generally followed on the farm, with especial reference to the week during which the cask was sent in.

"It is expected that a comparison of the feeding in the different dairies will give a very valuable insight into the influence of certain foods on the quality of butter.

"Invitations to take part in the shows are sent to dairies equal to turning out at least three casks of butter per week, and therefore likely to have a cask ready when the invitation reaches them. The butter sent is paid for at current market price. The authorities also defray cost of carriage from the station or port nearest to the dairy. As the same dairy will send in butter several times in the course of the year, great facilities will be afforded for ascertaining which are the best managed, or the reverse.

"The expenses attending these shows, which will be held at intervals of a fortnight during eight months of each year, are estimated at about £165 per month, and the Government grant for the current financial year is about £1,350."

This is all the help Government gives to the butter industry.

The following queries had to be answered by managers of competing dairies, with special reference to the show of December 2nd, 1889:—

1. How many pounds of sweet milk are daily made into butter in your dairy?
2. From how many cows is the milk drawn?
3. How many of these cows have calved since August 1st, 1889?
4. How many pounds of butter, of the same description as the sample now sent in, are made in the dairy daily?
5. Is the butter now sent in the produce of one day's churning? If so, which day? Or, of several days' churning? If so, which days?
6. How many pounds of milk were used to one pound of butter on the days referred to in query 5?
7. Is the milk set to cream in tubs? or pans? And of what kind? Are the tin pails set to cool in water without ice?

Butter Making.

or in water with ice? After how many hours is it skimmed? Is the milk churned?

8. Is a separator used? Is the milk warmed before being put into the separator? If so, to how many degrees of heat (Réaumur)? Is the milk cooled off at once after coming from the separator? If so, how? To what temperature? How much per cent. of cream is taken off?

9. Is saltpetre used? If so, how much to 100lb. of milk? or to 100lb. of cream?

10. With reference to souring cream, at what temperature does this begin? and terminate? How many hours did the cream stand? Is any ingredient used? If so, how is it prepared?

11. With reference to churning and kneading, at what temperature does churning begin? and terminate? How many minutes did the churning occupy? Is the butter when taken out washed in water? Is it washed a second time? How much salt is used per 1lb. of butter? How often is the butter kneaded after salting? How many hours does the butter remain between salting and final kneading? At what temperature is the butter kept between each time of pressing?

12. Is the dairy satisfied with the quality of its butter? If not, are you acquainted with the nature of its defects? Was the butter merchant satisfied with the last consignment? If not, of what did he complain?

13. With reference to feeding, especially for manor farms, but may be answered by other dairies. Food for new milch cows? Food for old milch cows? Amount per day per cow of the following food stuffs:—Corn, bran, oilcake, turnips, carrots, &c., turnip leaves, cabbage leaves, mangel leaves, ensilage, hay, straw, other food stuffs?

Danish butter stands very high in the English market, competing on equal ground with our own, and sometimes eclipsing the latter in price; Danish bacon, too, which is improving yearly, is equal to any except the very best qualities produced in England and Ireland.

The breed of pigs in Denmark is not usually Danish at all; on the contrary, the original animals came principally from Yorkshire and Berkshire. This is curious in itself. Denmark imports our pigs, breeds from them, fattens them, sends them back to us as bacon, and still secures a profit!

The pig trade, concurrently with the butter trade, has increased enormously in Denmark. In Copenhagen every morning the pig market is quite a feature in the day's proceedings. Carts laden with the carcasses arrive from the country or the station at very early hours, until the market-place is quite full, and the babel of voices tremendous. The costumes of the country folk are often very quaint, and one cannot but be struck by the good taste in colour often displayed by foreign peasants. Some of their silver ornaments, too, are very handsome, and so much prized, that their owners are quite insulted should a stranger offer to buy them.

This pig market is altogether a quaint scene, with its curious double windowed shops as a background. These double shops are very peculiar. The bottom one is half below the surface of the pavement, and the customer requires to go down a few steps to gain admittance. The top shop is immediately above the lower one, the windows literally adjoining, and the customer to gain admittance must go up steps at the other side. The result is striking; while in the lower half pork sausages or saddlery are exhibited for sale, dainty bonnets and pretty laces occupy the upper storey. Copenhagen is not satisfied with this extraordinary display of glass

Butter Making.

windows, for between the shops, dressmakers and glovers put little glass cases displaying their wares. The dressmakers' dolls are the most perfect models of costumes possible, and marvels of minute detail. With such a quaint background and such pretty costumes, the pig market becomes as picturesque a scene as an artist's eye can wish to gaze upon, and while it is picturesque it is also remunerative.

It is not by making butter alone that we English might earn money, but by rearing pigs on the milk left from the butter-making. Pig-rearing under such circumstances is an extremely profitable trade. Danish money-making does not stop at butter and pigs however, for Denmark makes £400,000 a year out of her egg export alone. England's import of eggs is about half a million a day, paid for with England's gold!

The British labourer has never excelled in rearing fowls, and yet it is on a small scale that fowls pay best, as the peasants of Denmark, Hungary, Belgium, France, and Russia have long since discovered. It is these countries which supply us with eggs, eggs not obtained from large farms at all, but from the village folk with their half-dozen fowls or so. These cottagers sell them to the egg collectors, who are continually going their rounds, and when they have obtained a sufficient number, they pack them securely in boxes and send them to England.

Denmark alone makes £8,456,434 a year out of England from butter, bacon, and eggs.

If Danes can produce these articles at a profit, why cannot we English? The climate of England is the same, and our geographical position better. In January, 1893, Denmark was so ice-bound that Elsinore, in the north, was the only port open for some weeks, during which period the butter was actually sent across to Sweden, from whence it travelled for a couple of days to Trondheim, and was then shipped over to England. The soil of England is better, too, than that of Denmark; but, alas! the enterprise is lacking, and there is no co-operation. Our farmers have unfortunately not yet realised that they are losing their trade, ruining themselves and their landlords, and until they do so nothing can be done, while the money earned by English manufacturers will necessarily be expended in foreign countries for England's foods. Her towns will increase, and her pastoral lands lie idle.

Passing through Copenhagen lately, our interest in butter was excited by some startling figures divulged at a large dinner party. Everyone at table drank the health of the "representatives of England which is doing so much to enrich Denmark." We became interested at what appeared, to our uninitiated mind, a very droll toast, and eagerly listened to a few details. Desirous of knowing more of this money-making butter business, through the kindness of Mr. Busck, who has been such a friend to Danish farmers, we were enabled to see over a butter factory.

These butter factories, of which there are about 1200, are scattered all over Denmark. The largest of them receives milk from more than 1000 cows daily. There are considerably above a million cows

Butter Making.

in the country, and yet there are only two millions human beings.

The average price paid to the farmers for milk is about 5d. a gallon, or for butter-making 3½d., and the skim milk is returned, but the value of the milk is more often rated by weight, which varies according to the amount of fat it contains; therefore all temptation to adulterate is done away with. The average price realised for butter is 9½d. a pound, the Danish pund being a trifle heavier than our own (1·102 lb. avoirdupois).

The market price of butter is regulated by a committee in Copenhagen, composed of a chairman elected by the Association of Wholesale Dealers, four of the largest butter exporters, a local dealer, a butter broker, and a dairy farmer representing the Zealand Co-operative Agricultural Society. This committee meets every Thursday to fix the wholesale price of butter for the ensuing week after taking the quotations of foreign markets into consideration.

The farmers are generally partners in the factories, and divide the profits, which depend entirely on the price the butter fetches in England. As all the butter factories are worked on the same principle, the one we visited, and are about to describe, gives a very good idea of what is being done so successfully throughout the whole country.

The manufactory lies a little outside the town, and thither we went about 9 p.m. At that hour the milk arrives from the country. The cows are milked at the farms about five o'clock, and after the milk has been thoroughly cooled it is sent off by cart or rail to the factory. The latter does not give special rates.

The Copenhagen Milk Supply Company purchases milk from about fifty different farmers, owning among them between four and five thousand cows. These cows are visited fortnightly by a veterinary surgeon, and if any disease breaks out between the visits the farmer must immediately report the same to the Company, which pays for the milk at the same rate as usual and then throws it away. By this plan the farmer has nothing to fear by telling the truth about the condition of his cows, and the spread of disease is avoided.

A pledge, of which the following is a copy, is signed by the contractors :—

"I, the undersigned contractor to the Copenhagen Milk Supply Company, pledge myself herewith, to the best of my ability, to inquire into every case of infectious disease occurring either upon my farm or among the people employed in working for me, and to report every case of the above kind immediately to the Company."

In return the Company bind themselves as follows :—

"The highest price in the market will be paid for the milk from such farms as usual, if the notice is given in time to prevent any of it from being sold."

In consequence of all these precautions there is guarantee that the stock, at any rate, is healthy.

It is well known by scientific and medical men that tubercular disease in the cow may be conveyed to a human subject by means of its milk, and that tuberculosis and consumption are identical. The ordinary term consumption is usually confined to tuberculosis of the lung, while tuberculosis refers to the disease in general, regardless of its seat. Further, milk is a very frequent cause of communicating diphtheria, scarlet fever, measles, enteric fever, and all zymotic diseases. It is therefore necessary to see that no one milking or attending to cows ever comes in contact with any of these diseases, and to avoid this the Company pays its *employés* full wages and keeps them on if they have been exposed to infection. Should a case of infectious disease appear among any of the farm *employés*, the farmer must at once report the fact to the Company and withhold the milk, which will nevertheless be paid for as usual, if these conditions are complied with.

During the summer months it is compulsory for the cattle to be fed out of doors, and the following are the regulations for contracts :—

NEWEST REGULATIONS FOR CONTRACTORS.

FEEDING AND MANAGEMENT.

1. The food of the cows must be of such a nature and quality that no bad taste or taint may be imparted to the milk by it.

    (*a*) Brewers' grain and all similar refuse from distilleries are strictly forbidden, as also is every kind of fodder which is not fresh and in good condition.
    (*b*) Turnips, kohlrabies, and rutabaga are absolutely forbidden; no kind of turnip leaves may be used.
    (*c*) Carrots and sugar beets (mangolds) are permitted up to half a bushel per cow, but only when at least 7lb. of corn, bran, and cake are to be given along with them. Cows supplying infant milk may get

carrots, but never more than a quarter of a bushel per head.

(d) Oilcake.—Rape seed cake is the only oil cake which may be used. 1½lb. is the furthest limit, along with at least 5lb. corn and bran. Infant milk cows must not receive any cake.

(e) The proportions in which the different kinds of food are to be given must be arranged with the company before the contractor commences to supply milk.

2. Stall feeding in summer will not be permitted under any circumstances. The cows must be fed in the open air upon clover and grass. Vetches are forbidden. In a case of necessity dry food or cut corn may be given, but on the field.

3. In autumn the cows must be clipped on the udder, tail, and hind quarters before being taken in.

4. Calving should be so regulated that the milk sent in during the months of September and October is not less than two-thirds of the largest quantity sent in in any other month.

5. The milk of cows newly calved must be withheld for twelve days after calving, and must not be less in quantity than three imperial quarts per day.

Autumn calving is a very important point, and one not sufficiently realised in England, for attention to it means that large quantities of milk are available in the winter when it would otherwise be scarce; consequently the supply of butter can be maintained during the colder months.

The cows of Denmark are usually bred in the country itself, and are small and reddish in colour. The Jutland cows on the contrary are generally black and white, and as a breed are better for fattening than milking. A full-grown milch cow of Danish breed weighs 800lb. or 1000lb , and will often yield,

Butter Making.

if well fed, from ten to twelve times its own weight in milk annually.

In the winter the cattle are stall fed, corn, bran, hay, and rape-seed cake being the chief foods. All must be of the very best quality. It has been proved that the better the food the more satisfactory the milk, and, therefore, the most paying. It may further be mentioned that all milk is valuable at the factories in proportion to its fatty properties and not in proportion to its quantity, which thus does away with all desire to adulterate it. Should the Company find the milk inferior, and therefore unfit for sale, they are entitled to refuse it without giving any compensation to the contractor. As a rule, however, all the regulations for cleanliness, good diet, ample ventilation, &c., are well attended to by the farmers with the most satisfactory results.

When milking it is essential that the greatest cleanliness should be observed. The milk is strained through a wire sieve covered with a clean woollen cloth. Immediately after milking, and during all seasons of the year, the milk must be cooled down with ice-water to 40° Fahr. About this the Company is most particular; 30lb. of ice have to be allowed for every 100lb. of milk, and a good supply of ice always kept in hand by the farmer. Much of the ice is collected from the ponds in winter, and therefore only costs the labour; but when this supply fails it has to be bought.

At most of the butter factories the cream only is delivered to the Company, the farmer keeping the milk for his household and animals, but as every little farmer in the country cannot afford a separator, sometimes all the milk is sent to the factory, or, in some cases, the factory cart fetches it, the amount of milk is entered in a book when weighed, and as much skimmed milk and butter as may be required by the farmer and his family are returned and debited to his account. Practice has enabled this entry system to be thoroughly and speedily worked.

As the Copenhagen factory supplies both milk and butter to the town, fresh milk is necessary as well as the cream.

The sweet milk arrives, as before said, in the evening, and every can is sampled by a woman whose sole duty is to taste milk (just as men taste tea or wine), and in a moment she is able to detect whether anything be amiss, in which case the can has to be put aside for analysis.

All the fresh milk that is approved of is passed through an enormous filter. This filter is filled with three layers of fine gravel, separated by perforated trays, and most carefully cleaned day by day. It is first washed with soda, rinsed with several clean waters, and then exposed to a temperature of 302° Fahr., which is sufficient to kill all bacteria. Mr. Busck invented this filter, and insists on having the filtering medium thoroughly sterilised each time it is used. Every drop of milk that comes to the factory is passed through it before being sold or put aside for butter.

One absolutely stands aghast before a bottle of débris collected from the filter, and thinks, with a shudder, that people generally—indeed always—

drink such filth in the London milk. Cow hair, human hair, fragments of corn, of wood, of wool, of anything and everything are filtered from the milk. And this is only the accumulation collected through the openings in the cans during their railway journey to Copenhagen.

While our milk is delivered at the London door in cans, with only half-closed lids, the Copenhagen milk is bottled and securely sealed down. The bottles are kept scrupulously clean. They are washed by machinery, first with soda and warm water by means of a revolving brush, and then with clean water. When filled with milk, they are corked down, a new cork being used each time, tied, sealed, and placed in ice all night, to be sent out for delivery in the morning.

The bottling arrangements are perfect, as indeed is everything in connection with the dairy. As the bottles are expensive they have to be paid for by whoever breaks them. Nearly 14,000 were broken last year; but then 3000 or 4000 go out every day for the morning delivery alone.

After the delivery of the milk, the rest is set aside for butter-making. It is placed in tall, straight, cylindrical tins and stood in ice for some hours for the cream to rise, when it is skimmed by hand, not by a separator. It then contains one per cent. of cream, and is sold as skimmed milk. When passed through a separator it rarely contains so much as half per cent. of cream, and is, therefore, only useful for animal feeding. When the cream has been skimmed from the milk in the cans, it is put into large tubs, and heated by hot air to 68° Fahr., so as to turn it sour quickly, for fresh cream will not make good butter. The cream stands in these huge tubs for twenty-four hours, and the tubs are so thick that it is necessary to keep up the temperature almost to 68° Fahr.

At the end of twenty-four hours the contents are usually sour enough to make good butter, but if not, a little "new-sour" of the day before has to be added. When the milk comes from all sorts of farms, and its condition varies, "new-sour" helps to maintain the standard. It is generally made by exposing the cream or milk to such heat as will develop the souring process. Uniformity in this matter is very essential to the uniformity in butter. Once the cream is ready in point of "ripeness," it is cooled down by being passed over tubes containing ice-water till it becomes 50° Fahr., which is the proper heat for churning. Indeed, M. Böggild, a great authority on butter-making, declares there is a great deficiency in the yield of butter if the cream is not cooled to from 46° to 56° Fahr. after separation.

Women are employed to make the butter. They are charmingly and suitably dressed in white, with short sleeves, large aprons, and pretty little white caps. On their feet they wear clogs, because the floor is always wet from the endless amount of washing continually going on. Everything is washed with hot water the moment it is laid aside; indeed, the whole factory is simply a marvel of cleanliness and order.

It is quite pleasant to see the cheerful faces

Butter Making.

of the women employed, and note the extreme neatness of their costumes. Theirs is a very healthy life, and they usually keep their situations for years, while the demand for places is far in excess of the vacancies.

The Danish butter-girls earn from 6s. to 12s. a week, and become so expert that it is quite interesting to see their dexterity in bottling, corking, tying up, washing, squeezing, weighing, &c. Women do a very large share of the work in the factory; in fact, all that does not entail carrying heavy weights, for which purpose men are employed, and also for driving the fifty milk vans used by the Company. Altogether about 250 people find employment in this one establishment, where they are well paid, lead a healthy life, and are looked after in sickness.

The cream, when it is put into the churns, smells sour and appears quite white, until the colouring matter is added, without which the butter would look like lard.

This colouring matter is called "smor faber," and is made from a root which grows in the East. Preparing it ready for use is another of the trades of Denmark, and is a further source of employment to the people. It is a lovely deep orange shade absolutely clear and like syrup, and one teaspoonful colours seventy-five kilos. of cream.

The churns are worked by machinery, and it takes about half an hour to make a large churn of butter at a temperature of 10 Cel. They are usually half full, never more than two-thirds, and the Holstein churn is the favourite throughout the country. It is an upright churn of wood, with a large opening over which the cover is fitted to receive the thermometer. The cream revolves on a wooden frame worked on an upright shaft. It is a very simple churn, so simple that it can be easily taken to pieces and cleaned.

One girl is able to look after three churns at the same time. They have to be very carefully watched and the temperature kept exact. The churn must be stopped the moment the butter is ready, otherwise it may be easily spoiled by being "overworked."

It takes about 4lb. of cream to turn out 1lb. of butter. Of course rich cream yields more; but this is the average when milk is used from many different farms.

The girl knows the moment the butter is ready by looking at the particles hanging to a stick suspended in the churn.

The butter in Denmark is seldom washed, it being believed that it loses its fine aroma thereby. Where it is washed, the strainer holding the mass is merely passed through a tub containing water which has been thoroughly boiled, and the water thus passing over the butter clears away any particles of buttermilk without washing the butter too much. When taken from the churn the milk is usually only shaken out of the butter through a sieve; then it is laid on huge wooden troughs, where scrupulously clean girls knead the first milk out of it with their hands. Then it is passed on to a "machine butter-worker," where it is further manipulated by wooden hands. This accomplished, dry salt is dredged over it.

Butter Making.   23

About 30 grammes, or 1 to 1½ oz. of salt to 1 kilo. (2lb.) of butter. Butter for distant export requires a good deal more salt than this, and butter for the colonies, that has to be packed up in tins, is still more salted, and also compressed before packing.

Having removed all the superfluous milk from the butter, great care being taken not to overwork it and thereby make it soft and greasy, and salted it to the right amount, the butter is all carefully weighed and entered in a book. It is marvellous to see the skill of these girls in weighing. They can nearly always pick up the exact pound or kilo. with their two wooden ladles. It is the exception, and not the rule, for them to have to add or deduct from the pat in the scale.

Butter for the town is packed in pretty 1lb. china pots, and passed on to another girl, who smooths it down before putting on the dairy stamp. These pots are returned by the residents when emptied, or charged for if kept or broken. Butter is usually served at table in them in Denmark.

Besides the supply of milk and cream sold from this factory, 400lb. to 800lb. of butter are made daily. About half of this is consumed by the town, and the remainder is packed for exportation.

The best sweet milk is delivered to the town in glass bottles, as explained before; the skimmed milk is sold very cheaply to the poor from large cans which are carried round the town in carts. The milk is drawn off by a tap, and as the can is sealed up before leaving the factory, the milk cannot be tampered with in any way. Buttermilk is sold separately. Besides all this, a large quantity of milk is given away every day for the children in the hospitals, or sold to public institutions at a reduced rate.

The milk is sold by the Company at the following prices:—

	Per gallon. s. d.		Per gallon. s. d.
Sweet milk	0 10	Infants' milk	1 0
Buttermilk	0 5	No. 1 cream	5 0
Half-skimmed milk	0 5	No. 2 cream	3 0

The half-skimmed milk, so much used by the poor, freed from all impurities, costs five farthings per quart, and this cheap rate actually leaves a slight profit after all the care and time bestowed on its transport, &c.

From all this it will be seen that this is indeed a model dairy, and it has received the sincere flattery of imitation. Dairies on the same principle are in working order in Paris, Berlin, St. Petersburg, Amsterdam, Stockholm, &c.

Its butter, milk, and cream are all excellent. It gives freely to the poor, and even then it always pays the five per cent. promised in its prospectus!

Besides this, it provides work for an astounding number of persons; not only is the farmer with his several hundred cows benefited, but the crofter as well, for he sends the milk of his one, or, it may be, two cows to the factory also. Then there are the labourers, the butter-makers, carmen, &c. Hundreds are making a living, the town is getting good and cheap milk and butter, and the shareholders receive their dividends. What more could be wanted?

From M. Böggild's article on co-operative dairies I quote the following, which was one of the first set of rules made.

ARTICLES OF ASSOCIATION.

Par. 1.

Object of Association.—The object of the co-operative association is to erect a dairy and to provide the members with the highest possible profit on their cows, by separating the milk in centrifugal separators and manufacturing the cream into butter for sale, while the separated milk shall be made into sufficient skim-milk cheese to supply the requirements of the members and the neighbourhood, and the remaining separated milk, buttermilk, and whey shall be sold to the members at a fair price.

Par. 2.

Admittance of Members.—Any person holding milch cows may be admitted to the association, provided two-thirds of the members vote in favour of his admittance, but any member admitted after the association has begun its operations shall pay an entrance fee of 5s. 6d. per cow. Every member has as many votes as he has cows.

Par. 3.

Directorate.—The directorate of the association shall be elected by the members, and shall consist of five directors, who shall choose from among themselves a chairman, a secretary, and a treasurer, but these three offices must never be combined in one and the same person. The directorate shall represent the interests of the individual members in all matters concerning the association, and the signature of the directorate is absolutely binding on the association. One director shall retire every year; in the first five years of the association he shall retire by ballot, but afterwards in rotation; he is eligible for re-election. The directors receive no remuneration, but they may employ a book-keeper, whose annual salary shall be at the rate of 6d. per cow, and they have the right to take any sums from the funds of the dairy for the payment of expenses incurred on behalf of the association.

Par. 4.

General Meeting. — The highest authority is vested in the general meeting, which shall be regularly held in the month of February, when every question at issue between the directorate and the members, or between members, shall be finally settled. At this meeting the directorate shall present the account and balance-sheet of the previous year, and a statement of the proposed operations for the ensuing year. The meeting shall proceed to the election of a new director, an accountant, and an auditor (the auditing shall be carried out by two members of the association, one of whom shall retire each year). An extraordinary general meeting may be called whenever the directors consider necessary, or when three-fourths of the members hand in a written request to that effect. No general meeting shall be valid unless at least two days' notice thereof has been given in writing or printing to every member, together with a list of the subjects to be discussed. Members can introduce special subjects, but a decision can only be taken thereon when such subjects have been formally recognised, otherwise the decision must be deferred till the next meeting. Alterations in, or additions to, the articles of association, and resolutions to liquidate the association can only be carried when three-fourths of the total votes are recorded in favour thereof. All other matters and election of officers shall be carried by a simple majority.

Par. 5.

Loan for Erection of Dairy.—The directorate is authorised to contract a loan for the erection of the dairy and purchase of plant. For the payment of this loan every member is held liable in the proportion to the number of his cows, until the loan has been repaid.

Par. 6.

Withdrawal of Members.—When a farm belonging to a member is sold, or otherwise transferred, the share in the dairy is sold therewith, provided that the new owner or tenant will accept all the rights and duties of his predecessor in respect to the dairy. In other cases the association shall pay to the outgoing member, or his heirs, or his creditors, one half only of the amount of his share. Until the debt on the dairy is paid off a member can only withdraw on giving up his farm. A member who desires to with-

Butter Making. 27

draw must give three months' notice to the directorate, and even then he shall only have a right to receive half the amount of his share. Any member expelled by a vote at the general meeting forfeits all claims on the dairy.

Par. 7.

Dairyman.—The directorate may engage a dairyman, who shall manage the operations of the dairy and keep all the books with the exception of the cash book and minute book. The dairyman shall engage, pay, and board the assistants; of the latter there shall be at least one person experienced in dairying, and understanding the preparation of butter, and at least one must be acquainted with the management of the machines. The dairyman shall receive a small fixed salary quarterly, as well as free lodging, with a garden, light and firing, and sufficient butter and cheese to meet the requirements of himself and his family; he shall also receive a commission on every hundred pounds of butter sold at a satisfactory price.

Par. 8.

Payment for Milk.—The milk shall be paid for according to its fat contents, which shall be determined by the dairyman; the milk will be weighed on its arrival at the dairy.

Par. 9.

Buttermilk and Separated Milk.—In proportion to the quantity of milk he delivers every member is bound to take back the buttermilk and separated milk, and he shall pay for these by-products at the rate of one öre per lb. until the debt on the dairy is fully paid off. Later, the general meeting will decide every year at what price these by-products shall be sold to members, but as a rule the actual value shall be paid. Cheese must only be made in such quantities as will return the actual value of the milk used for the purpose.

Par. 10.

Profits and Losses under Paragraphs 8 and 9.—Any balance accruing under paragraphs 8 and 9 shall be devoted to covering the expenses of working and maintenance, while all the remainder is to be used in payment of the interest on, and the extinction of, the debt of the dairy. Losses on the other hand shall be borne by the members, each in proportion to the sum representing the quantity of new milk he has delivered.

Par. 11.

Annual Profits.—As soon as the debt on the dairy is paid off, the chairman, accountant, and dairyman shall take an inventory of the society's assets. The total value thereof shall be apportioned as shares among the members in proportion to the quantity of milk each has delivered since the foundation of the dairy. Thereafter the yearly profits are to be divided in such a way that in the first place five per cent. is paid on every share, and the remainder is to be distributed in proportion to the value representing the milk delivered by each member during the previous year.

Par. 12.

Transport of Milk to Dairy.—The dairy shall provide and maintain the necessary transport churns, and shall undertake the transport of the milk to the dairy. If a member supplies less than 100 lb. of milk daily, he must take the milk to the nearest high road along which the dairy cart runs. Quantities exceeding 100 lb. will be fetched from the member's house, but he must keep the private road in good condition. The milk churns must be ready for delivery at the time fixed for the cart to call.

Par. 13.

Transport Churns must be clean—Milk must be fresh and good.— Every member must keep his transport churns perfectly clean, and he must see that the milking is properly carried out, that all the milk is immediately passed through a strainer into the churns, and that the latter are placed in cold water which is changed when necessary. Milk from sick cows must not be sent to the dairy, and no milk must be sent until five days have elapsed after calving. It is the duty of the dairyman, when weighing the milk at the dairy, to see that it is fresh and good. If the churns are not clean or the milk not sweet, the dairyman shall on the first occasion give notice in writing to the member concerned. If these faults are not at once remedied the dairyman may refuse to receive the milk, and if the cans are repeatedly found to be improperly cleaned the member concerned shall be fined each time 2s. 3d. for every cow he holds. Members are not allowed to offer butter or cheese for sale, nor are they permitted to sell their milk to other dairies. But they may keep a sufficient quantity of milk to meet the requirements of their families, and they may give away or sell milk to the peasants in the neighbourhood who keep no cows, provided the interests of the association are not thereby injured. The members have the right to obtain butter for their families from the dairy at a price per pound equal to that which the dairy is receiving for the product.

Par. 14.

Feeding of Cows.—Members are bound to feed their cattle in such a way that the milk possesses no flavour which is likely to depreciate the quality of the butter. Cabbage, turnip tops, and kohlrabi tops must never be given to the cows. Turnips, kohlrabi, potatoes, rye, vetches, beans, as well as sunflower seed-cake, earth-nut cake, and such foods are not absolutely prohibited, but when such questionable or doubtful feeding materials are given to milch cows the member using them must notify the fact to the dairyman, in order that special attention may be given to the quality of the milk. If the milk, or cream, or butter is detrimentally flavoured thereby, it is the duty of the dairyman to notify the fact to the member concerned, and if no improvement is observed the dairyman may refuse to receive the milk. The chairman of the dairy and the dairyman can at any time prohibit the use of any fodder considered unsatisfactory. Any member who infringes such a prohibition shall be fined from 2s. 3d. to 11s. per cow, and pay for any damage or loss he may have occasioned as estimated by the chairman, accountant, and dairyman.

Par. 15.

Purchase of Fodder, Grasses, &c.—In order that the members may obtain cheap and good feeding materials the directorate shall arrange for the purchase of such materials in bulk, and shall undertake the delivery of same to the members. In order to ensure that the butter may at all times have a satisfactory aroma, every member is bound to purchase as much rape cake as shall furnish at least 1 lb. of the cake daily to every cow during the winter. Finally, the directorate shall seek by every means to get the members to adopt a good, rational, and economical system of feeding their cows, by arranging for the purchase and delivery of grass seeds, &c., so that such grasses and plants may be cultivated as shall have a beneficial influence on the quality of the butter.

Par. 16.

Inspection of Members' Farms and Stock.—It shall be the duty and right of the directorate and of the dairyman, whenever they think fit, to visit the members' farms and to inspect the sheds, fodder lofts, and troughs, fields, milking sheds, &c., and the members must give them all necessary help and information. If it is afterwards found that a member has concealed anything, or given false information, he shall be fined from 2*s.* 3*d.* to 11*s.* per cow, and make good any loss or damage he may have occasioned.

Par. 17.

Infectious Diseases.—In order that no infectious disease may be spread through the dairy, and that the separated milk may be of the greatest use to the members, the separated milk shall always be heated at the dairy in order to preserve it. If an infectious disease breaks out in the family, or among the stock of a member, the member must immediately cease to deliver milk at the dairy until the disease has disappeared and his farm has been properly disinfected. In the event of sickness among the staff of the dairy the dairyman shall have the sick person removed immediately, and the dairy must be disinfected. Any infringement of this clause shall be punished by a fine up to £5.

Par. 18.

Duties of Directorate.—It is the duty of the directorate to supervise the work of the dairyman and to take care that the dairy, together with the machinery and plant, is at all times in proper working order. It is especially the duty of the directorate, in the spring of each year, to see that the dairy and all machinery, &c., is thoroughly overhauled and repaired, so that the work may proceed in good order during the hot and busy summer season. Every spring, after the repairs have been carried out, the chairman, accountant, and dairyman shall take stock of all the plant and fittings in the dairy, so that the members may have an estimate of the value of the property, and ascertain whether there has been any depreciation.

Butter Making. 31

Par. 19.

Investment of Balance.—It is the duty of the directorate to see at all times that the balance in cash is invested in some suitable manner for the benefit of the association. Once a month there shall be a settlement of the amounts due to the members for milk, after deducting the value of butter, &c., which they may have received from the dairy. The distribution of dividends and profits is made once a year after the accounts have been made up and the general meeting held.

Par. 20.

All matters not provided for in these articles must be brought before the general meeting, which alone can make changes in or additions to these provisions.

Danish butter has, within the last year, met with a rival in the English market; but that rival is not England herself, but her colonies.

Owing to the difference of season at the Antipodes, the winter butter coming to us from Australia and New Zealand is grass-fed. The Danish winter butter is fodder-fed, and grass butter is naturally richer and of better quality than stall-fed. Last winter's consignment of colonial butter reduced the Danish a penny a pound; but still there seems plenty of room for them both, although the results may not be quite so profitable to Denmark as formerly.

The P. and O. steamer *Ballarat* entered the Royal Albert Docks one day with a hundred tons of butter from New South Wales, and six hundred tons from Victoria; that is to say, about £68,000 worth!

Owing to the kindness of Sir Thomas Sutherland I am able to give the following figures. The largest shipment of butter by P. and O. steamer from Australia was 33,073 packages, each weighing ½ cwt., or 827 tons. The space occupied in the ship was about 1,500 tons (or 40 cubic feet).

Butter is generally shipped from the colonies about September or October (although in 1893 it commenced as early as July), and, as a rule, continues to arrive until the end of April.

The total quantity of butter sent from the colonies by the Orient and P. and O. steamers during the winters of 1893-94 amounted to upwards of 8,000 tons (of 20 cwt.), since which time even larger quantities have been shipped, as well as large consignments of bacon. The first impetus to the industry was a subsidy given to the dairy farmers by the Victorian Government on all butter exported; but now New South Wales, South Australia, and Tasmania are shipping large quantities without any Government assistance.

In January, 1895, £381,818 worth of butter arrived from the colonies! This butter, having to accomplish a voyage of 12,000 miles, can only be carried in refrigerating chambers specially constructed, and worked at large expense, an even temperature from 32 to 37 degrees having to be maintained. This is no easy matter, when ships are navigating the Red Sea and the Indian Ocean at the hottest time of the year. If the work were not done with the utmost possible care and circumspection, it would not be possible for the butter to arrive in a marketable condition.

Thus we see Australian butter requires specially

Butter Making

prepared rooms for its transport; the Danish butter, on the contrary, comes over in ordinary ships, without ice. But the Danes are very particular that their produce should be delivered in first-class condition, and if there be any doubt on this point, it is analysed by the representative of the Danish Agricultural Society, who lives in London.

The Australians are so delighted with their great financial success, owing to the splendid market they have found in England for their butter, that they are making arrangements for extending the business more rapidly. The Victorian Government, in May, 1895, entered into arrangements with the Blue Anchor and Aberdeen lines of steamers for a regular service to England, in order to transport butter, bacon, &c. This is the success of two or three years!

Another lesson we might learn from Denmark is mentioned by Sir Francis Denys, in his report on the Control of the Danish Meat Supply. He tells us that their regulations are not only sanitary but economic. The cattle, sheep, and swine have to undergo a rigid veterinary examination both before and after they are slaughtered. Before meat can be removed from the slaughter-house it must be officially stamped as "first or second class food." Some unscrupulous butchers tried to efface this stamp by cutting it out, or chemically removing it, and replacing "first" for "second class"; but they were summarily dealt with, and a fine of £110 imposed, which has effectually put a stop to their tricks.

It is not only in Denmark that meat is marked (although it is done there for quality), but in Italy, the United States, the Netherlands, Belgium, and Germany. A Select Committee in the House of Lords is beginning to see the advisability of this plan (at present only adopted in England to distinguish the meat killed for the use of the Jews), which would enable the buyer to ascertain whether it is English, foreign, or colonial meat his unscrupulous butcher passes off as "the best English" at the best English prices. Perhaps in time our Government will superintend the slaughter-house, and mark the meat as "first or second class," as is the custom in Denmark. That little country is now beginning to send us large supplies of butchers' meat, and a Bill was brought forward in November, 1893, by the Minister of the Interior, in the "Folkething," authorising him to direct official veterinary inspection to be made of all the consignments before they are packed for England, in order to secure the export of none but the best quality.

The Danes are very careful concerning their food supplies, and proportionally successful in their gains.

CHAPTER II.

HAVING described, as fully as I am able, what Denmark has done, and is doing in the matter of dairy produce, let me now turn to our own country.

After going thoroughly into the subject, I have come to the conclusion that *England has forgotten the art of butter-making.*

If such be the case, and few, I imagine, will be found to dispute my contention, this question then naturally arises, "Would not the British farmer be acting wisely if he strove to regain his former supremacy as producer of the finest milk, cream, butter, cheese, bacon, poultry, and eggs in the world?"

That he has through indifference lost that high position is undoubted, and it is for him and all who have the welfare of this "tight little island" at heart to consider whether CO-OPERATION—which has succeeded so admirably in Denmark that she can draw in fair exchange millions of pounds sterling every year from England—would not be the best means of compassing wealth and reputation for Great Britain and Ireland. *Co-operation means uniformity* of quality in the articles previously mentioned at the smallest possible cost; while uniformity in good produce means an ever *increasing and extending market.*

Why do we hear so constantly that English butter does not pay? Simply because there is now *no dependence to be placed upon it.* The wholesale dealer, like the village shopkeeper, must buy goods on which he can rely.

"I cannot imagine," said one of the latter class quite recently, "what the English farmers are thinking about. I have just bought a lot of Dorset at the rate of 9s. the 12lb., while I pay 1s. per pound for Danish, *which we always use* ourselves. It is precisely the same with Irish butter, which comes over in lumps weighing six or eight pounds. One week it is beautiful, no one need desire better; the next it is just as bad. The Danish is a little salt, but we always know what we are going to get."

Yes; people must know what they are "going to get," or they will cease to buy, and the above sentence puts in a nutshell why Danish butter is pushing English out of the market.

If English people will only resolve to buy English butter, and see that each pound is properly marked, then our own butter would soon find a sale, and good factories would immediately spring up on all sides. The old trade would be revived, agricultural England might look up again, and the cry of depression be lost in the clamorous sounds of exultation.

The owner of one of the largest dairies in England, which sells widely in its own county, thinking to enlarge his trade (which he started from philanthropic principles) and thereby encourage the younger men to stay on their own land, asked one of the largest West End shopkeepers if he would contract to take a certain supply of butter, packed according to regulation. " Yes," replied the West End dealer; " I will take it at 6½d. a pound! I cannot pay more, for I am never sure of English butter!"

Miss Smith-Dorien, who interests herself greatly in English dairying, and is taking an active part in the attempt to help British farmers, says: " Butter, bacon, poultry, eggs, honey, pork, and cheese, are commodities which formerly were largely produced, and bought and sold in our country in the days when it was:

> " *Farmers to the plough,*
> *Daughters to the mow,*
> *Wife to the cow,*
> *Son to the low.*

" The wife and daughters then carried their produce to the nearest market and sold it. Now, alas! it is:

> " *Farmer 'tally-ho!'*
> *Daughter piano,*
> *Wife silk and satin,*
> *Son Greek and Latin.*"

A bantering statement which has unfortunately a certain amount of truth underlying it.

At the present time, even if the farmers do send their produce to London, or any other large town, the want of uniformity in it causes customers to complain, and thus the wholesale merchants are compelled to import foreign produce, which at any rate does not vary in quality. Last year the import, as has been stated, of butter alone amounted to £13,470,419 !!!

Foreign merchants co-operate to import, while English agriculturists sit with folded hands and watch ruin coming upon them like an armed man. Co-operation on all sides is what is required, and Miss Smith-Dorien is right in wishing the wives of the large landed proprietors to form themselves into a committee, each district undertaking to rouse its own farmers, and encourage them in every way, by taking a personal interest in their tenants' dairy work.

By far the most important scheme for helping the agriculturists of England to rise to better things is the " National Agricultural Union," in which the Earl of Winchilsea takes a prominent place.

In December, 1892, a great agricultural conference was held in St. James's Hall, whereat that nobleman proposed a resolution to the effect that : " What was required was a National Agricultural Union, composed of all classes and persons concerned with the land." So began, only three years ago, what has grown to be an enormous project, the object of which is to secure the co-operation of all connected with the land, whether as owners, occupiers, or labourers, for the common good, and to promote and advance the best interests of agriculture; to frame and watch over measures affecting agricultural interests, and to take such action thereon, both in and out of Parliament, as may seem desirable for the benefit of agriculture.

The minimum annual subscriptions payable by members will be on the following basis :

	£	s.	d.
OWNERS OF LAND—Under 100 acres	0	5	0
From 100 to 500 acres	0	10	0
Over 500 acres	1	0	0
OCCUPIERS (not being owners)—Over 20 and under 100 acres	0	2	6
From 100 to 500 acres	0	5	0
Over 500 acres	0	10	0
LABOURERS and OCCUPIERS of 20 acres or less One Penny per Month, or	0	1	0
All other persons	0	2	6

Which statement shows that the scheme comprises not only landowners, but farmers and labourers. The great interests of the three classes are identical. Of course differences may arise as to the division of the profits, but that is a mere matter of detail; the great thing—the first step, in fact—is for the three classes to join together and bring back the profits, which at the present moment have saved anyone the trouble of distributing by disappearing altogether. To quote Lord Winchilsea, the objects of of the union are :

To frame such measures as may from time to time be needful in the agricultural interest ; to organise in every constituency a body of public opinion favourable to the return, without distinction of party, of candidates who support the programme of the union, and generally to promote the co-operation of all persons connected with the land, whether as owners, occupiers, or labourers, for the common good. Membership shall be open to all persons of whatever class who are interested in the land of the United Kingdom. The annual subscriptions payable by members I have fixed upon a basis which, of course, finds a place in the draft scheme ; but this point in connection with it I do rather press upon the attention of this meeting. I have made a sliding scale by which owners will be asked to contribute in proportion to the number of acres which we, as a union, shall assist in protecting from spoilation. I do not think that is unfair, because the part which each class will take in making this union a success must be rather a different one. They will all belong to it; but I make no secret of the fact that we cannot carry on this union without money.

In time the N.A.U. hopes to establish a branch in every group of parishes.

The Agricultural Union is not political—that is to say, it belongs to no party, and is only political inasmuch as it wants Parliament to do a great deal to help it.

Lord Winchilsea adds :

There are nearly 200 members nominally representing the agricultural interest in Parliament, and with the aid of their constituents we want to form them into an agricultural party in the House of Commons. In some things Parliament can help us, in others we must rely upon ourselves.

The question of protection and the question of bimetallism, although most important, we put aside for the present—we are neither protectionists nor free traders; we are not, in fact, committed to any party *politics*, our one object being to induce the farmers to try and work together for their mutual good.

The more we inquire into the actual causes which are continually displacing a larger and larger proportion of English-grown produce from the home market, and allowing its place to be usurped by goods of foreign origin, the more clear it becomes that the secret of the foreigner's success, and our failure, is to be found in the fact that he has been prompt to avail himself of that most potent of all the weapons with which modern competition can be carried on—namely, co-operation and combination—whereas, up to the present moment, our own farmers have persisted in shutting their eyes to the absolute necessity for this new departure. "Combination between all classes connected with land in order to advance their common interests" is the great object of the N.A.U., but it would be impossible now to discuss the manner in which the introduction of this great principle will enable agriculture to obtain justice from the Legislature in the form of a redistribution of local burdens, relief from excessive or preferential railway rates, and in other directions. Here and now we are concerned with its application to the growth, preparation, collection, distribution, and marketing of home agricultural produce. Very early in the history of the N.A.U. the close attention of the council, and of both the important congresses which have been held under its auspices, was directed to this all-important point, and a strong committee has been engaged in working up the question, in consultation with experts. The result of their labours may be thus briefly summarised :

It is proposed to launch in the autumn a co-operative association, under strong central management, which will undertake the duty of providing efficient and reliable salesmen of its own in the principal wholesale markets, avoiding retail dealing, and confining its operations to wholesale transactions. It will also establish its own collecting depôts in the country, where agricultural produce intended for consignment to the company's salesmen can be sent, and where, if necessary, it can be packed and prepared in such a manner as to fit it for the market and sent on in such quantities as will enable the association to claim from the railway companies the same rates which they now accord to foreign produce.

The work of this central association must be supplemented by improved means of collecting produce locally and conveying it to the depots, and, of course, as time goes on, by the establishment of central creameries, butter factories, *abattoirs*, and all the well-known methods so long and successfully adopted abroad, by which individual producers are made to concentrate their energies for the joint production of an excellent and marketable article. It is here that the N.A.U., with its 500 branches, forty rural councils, and complete organisation, will be of the most enormous assistance, by setting on foot local societies in connection with its branches, in order to supplement the work of the central association, and to enable its members to take advantage of the help which that will provide. Evidence is daily forthcoming of the absolute necessity which exists that some step of this kind shall immediately be taken, and it is to be hoped that, now that action is contemplated under such favourable auspices, every landowner and tenant farmer will support the association by taking shares in it, and, what is even more important, by being ready to take his part, when the time comes, in the various local organisations which will be its

proper feeders, and essential to the completion of the great work
which is thus to be undertaken.

The company would be agents, and would have their own
salesmen in the market. It would establish stalls in London,
Birmingham, &c., and have depôts in the country from which it
could procure meat, butter, cheese, eggs, and poultry, which are now
produced in a haphazard way and sold at a loss, or at very little profit.

The committee has formed a valuable scheme for getting over
these and many other kindred difficulties. The principle on
which they are wisely going is to avoid retail dealing; to establish
themselves as wholesale agents in order that the farmers may
have reliable salesmen in the markets.

Speaking of the N.A.U., Lord Winchilsea said :

That, whereas the income of the country is now about
£1,000,000,000 a year, the income of land and houses is only
about £160,000,000, or one-sixth, but this one-sixth has to pay
practically the whole of the local taxation of the country. The
farmers have to pay rates for making the roads which other people
use; just the same with the education rate. Charges which, like
the poor rate, education rate, highway rate, and police rate,
correspond to national duties and requirements ought to be
equally distributed over the national income, and ought not to
fall on one-sixth of it alone.

We desire to reduce all excessive railway rates, or to abolish
those preferential ones which the companies now grant to foreign
produce—a very grave question.

It is an undoubted fact that foreign produce is permitted to
come into this country at a cheaper rate than that at which our
own is allowed to travel along the same lines. What a shame! is
naturally the first exclamation, and so undoubtedly it is, for we
have no right to extend advantages to foreigners which we do not
give to our own producers. But there is another side to the
question. Foreign dairy produce landed at Southampton is
brought up to London at 10*s*. a ton; English dairy produce
coming from the same town to the metropolis is charged 30*s*.
This fact sounds iniquitous, and yet what do the railway companies
say? They reply that the foreign consignment is regular; it
comes weekly—daily, in fact; it comes in bulk in large consignments; it comes *properly packed*, and in consequence of being a

Butter Making. 43.

regular trade, which complies with all our rules, it pays us much better to carry foreign produce at 10*s*. a ton than it does to receive three times that amount for English goods, a quantity of which will be sent one day, and none perhaps for a fortnight. When they are sent it is generally in small quantities, and always in oddly shaped cases and baskets, so badly packed that the butter is damaged, the eggs are broken, and our vans dirtied. The consigners of the package then expect us to pay them compensation for their own badly packed packages. This assertion is most serious. To think that we cannot even pack an egg without the chance of its breaking, while thousands of boxes arrive from Russia in which perhaps not one single egg is found to be cracked! Packing seems to be as necessary a subject for pondering over and learning as the great dairying question itself.

Lord Winchilsea, in the House of Lords, on one of the last days of May, supported Lord Jersey's motion for a Committee :

His Lordship pointed out that the object of the motion was not to induce the House to take any steps to place the foreigner in a position of inferiority in regard to the home producer, but to see whether the intention of the Legislature to place foreign and English goods precisely on the same level was being honestly and fairly carried out. The proper use of the word "similar" would also have to be considered. He would be satisfied if for similar services they could get similar rates. There could be no doubt that a great part of the discrepancy which they now suffered under was really brought about by the fact that the agriculturists and traders had not learned the great lesson of combination, by sending their goods to a centre where they could be properly packed and properly conveyed to the railway companies. He challenged any representative of the railway companies to say, if an association or society could be got to deliver goods to the railway companies properly packed, in regular quantities and at regular times, whether the railway companies would grant them the same rates which they granted to foreigners. If they would not, then behind that refusal lay the very thing the motion wanted to get at. They were entitled to protest against that form of protection which was the most odious of all—the protection of the foreigner at the expense of the home producer.

The question before the House, as Lord Winchilsea explained, lay really in a nutshell. Parliament undoubtedly intended by means of the proviso to put a stop to the preferential treatment of foreign produce by railway companies. The question is, has it succeeded? The railway companies contend that it has, but the universal opinion of traders and agriculturists is that it has not. It is in the interests of both that the point should be authoritatively cleared up, and the truth ascertained, by an impartial inquiry.

The most telling instance which Lord Winchilsea was able to give the House, of the deliberate manner in which the railway companies have set themselves to render nugatory the intentions of Parliament as expressed in the proviso, was to be found in the rates charged for the conveyance of foreign and English meat respectively from Liverpool to London. In the one case it is 25*s.* per ton, in the other 50*s.*, or exactly double. Seeing, however, that so manifest a violation of the Act could not be upheld, the railway company offered to carry English meat at the same rate as foreign—namely, 25*s.* per ton—"*provided it were delivered to them in consignments of not less than 20 tons at one time.*"

Now the quantity here selected, as Lord Winchilsea pointed out, is extremely significant. If, on the one hand, it had been a full truck load, which would be about 5 tons, or if, on the other, it had amounted to a full train load, which would be, say, 100 tons, the limit would have been intelligible; but 20 tons is far more than the one, and far less than the other. Why, then, was it selected? It is impossible to escape from the only logical conclusion, that the limit was fixed because it was known to be one to which no home producer could attain; that, therefore, the home producer would be compelled as before to send at the double, or 50*s.* rate; while the railway company would be able to plead that they were technically complying with the Act, because the services performed in the two cases were not "similar."

A practical suggestion for helping farmers was laid before the House of Commons in March, 1895, by Sir John Kinloch, M.P. for East Perthshire. It was as follows:

To ask the President of the Board of Agriculture if he has observed that, notwithstanding the great depression of agriculture

Butter Making.

in the United Kingdom, butter, cheese, and eggs to the value of nearly £23,000,000 were imported last year from abroad, the imports of butter having increased from £11,985,190 in 1892 to £13,470,419 in 1894, the increase on butter from Denmark alone for the same period amounting to £1,000,000.

Whether he has considered any means of encouraging the British agriculturists so to increase the production of home-made butter as to render unnecessary the large importation from foreign countries.

Whether the difficulty of distribution could be overcome by enabling farmers, under a cheap rate of postage, to send butter direct by parcel post to the customer.

And whether he will arrange with the Postmaster-General to facilitate the forwarding of butter under a special rate of 1d. per 17oz., so as to allow for the packing of one pound parcels.

To this the President of the Board of Agriculture and the Postmaster-General admitted "they were powerless to act in the matter." The railway monopolies hold the key to the situation.

The following programme is to be put before every Member of Parliament for an agricultural constituency by the N.A.U.:

1. To relieve agricultural land from the unfair share which it now bears of the local burdens of the country, by placing upon the whole national income charges which, like the poor rate, the highway rate, and the education rate, correspond to national duties and requirements.

2. To restrain railway companies from imposing excessive rates for the carriage of agricultural produce, and especially from granting rates which give a preference to foreign produce over our own.

3. To provide State-aided old-age pensions for working men.

4. To introduce such improvements into the Agricultural Holdings Act (1883) as may be necessary to give the tenant security for his improvements, taking good husbandry into account.

5. To extend the Merchandise Marks Act to food, and to strengthen the existing law which deals with adulteration.

6. Power to the Government, in the case of landlords who desire to create small holdings in suitable localities, to advance the money required to make the necessary buildings, roads, fences, &c., on moderate terms as to interest and repayment, and on the security of the holding.

On December 7, 1893, the above programme (with the exception of the last item, which there was not time to introduce) was placed in a series of resolutions—all of which it unanimously adopted—before the Agricultural Congress, the most representative agricultural gathering ever held in these Kingdoms, to which, though held under the auspices of the National Agricultural Union, all existing agricultural societies were invited to send representatives, among the delegates actually present being 250 agricultural labourers.

NOTE.—*The above is being placed before all candidates for agricultural constituencies, whether Liberal or Conservatives, with a view to the formation of a strong Agricultural Party in the new Parliament, and is being largely supported.*

One of the most delightful dairies in England is Blythwood, in Essex. Really the private property of Sir James Blyth, the owner of the famous herd of Jerseys, it is so beautifully managed, and the butter produced there is of such splendid quality, that it may be regarded as a regular model dairy, teaching a practical lesson.

The milk arrives from the farm in the afternoon, when it is immediately poured into the separator, where, at the rate of 7000 revolutions a minute, the milk and the cream run into different receptacles a moment or two later. The cream is allowed to sour before being used, although, as Miss Jacobs the head dairymaid explained, the milk *could* appear as butter in one hour from the time it arrived from the farm! The churn is worked by electricity. One

Butter Making. 47

pound of salt to a gallon of water being added. When the butter is ready, it is poured into a butter drier, one of the most delightful of modern inventions, because it entirely dispenses with the necessity of the butter being ever touched with the hand.

The following rules are given by Sir James Blyth in connection with his model dairy at Stansted, Essex :

GOLDEN RULES FOR A BUTTER-MAKING DAIRY.

Give the cows 2lb. to 3lb. of concentrated food daily when on the pastures.

See that they have access to pure water. That they are not worried by flies, or over-driven by boys, or hunted by dogs.

Add a Jersey or Guernsey or two to the herd; it will improve the butter. Milk regularly.

Insist upon the udders being wiped clean, and the milkers having clean hands and pails.

Never mix the milk of a newly-calved cow, or a very stale milker with that from the others.

Keep rock salt, or Spratt's salt rollers, in the manger.

Always clean out the manger after every meal.

Treat the animals with kindness: they will amply repay it.

Never dip the fingers in the pail when milking.

In winter never use swedes, turnips, or grains, sour ensilage, musty hay, barley straw, or an excessive quantity of oil cake.

Select such roots as carrots, parsnips and mangolds, the best hay, oat-straw, sweet grass, clover or vetch silage, oats, bran, middlings, maize-meal, cocoa-nut, decorticated cotton or palm-nut cake, cotton-seed meal, Thorley's cake, malt combs.

Carry the milk to the dairy while warm from the cow. It must not be allowed to cool, either for shallow or deep setting, before pouring into the setting vessels.

Strain it carefully.

For shallow setting, set in as cool a dairy as possible; for deep setting, set as near 40° F. as possible, giving a fall of at least 50°.

Take care that the setting vessels and the dairy are thoroughly sweet and clean, and the latter dry, free from draughts conveying foul smells, and without drains, trapped or otherwise.

In thundery weather use the Cooley system, setting as near 45° F. as possible, the milk being at 90° F. at least.

Skim with clean utensils.

Place the cream in a deep earthen vessel, and when adding subsequent skimmings, stir and mix the whole with a wooden stirrer.

In summer churn at least thrice weekly. In mid-winter once may be sufficient, but if the cream can be quickly ripened, twice is better.

Never add sour milk or whey to cream.

Before churning strain the cream, heat it in winter, never quickly, to 62° F., in summer cool it slowly to 58° F. In spring and autumn adopt 60° F.

Churn in a room as near 60° F. as possible, never in a very hot or very cold room.

Never fill the churn more than half full.

Churn at medium speed, 40 to 48 revolutions per minute, unless the new rapid type of churn is used.

Invariably use a thermometer, and take care that it is correct.

Press the vent and allow the escape of gas a few minutes after commencing.

Stop immediately the butter breaks, open the churn and add a little cold water.

Churn a few seconds gently, to allow the grains of butter to gather until they are as large as grains of wheat, then draw off the buttermilk through a strainer, and add clean cold water for washing.

Churn a few revolutions for this purpose, but so gently that the grains will not gather, and then draw off the water.

Repeat this operation three or four times until the water runs off clean; then make brine of the purest fine dry salt, and again wash the butter, allowing the brine to remain 10 to 30 minutes before drawing off.

Draw off all the moisture possible.

Remove the butter to the worker, and there express the remaining moisture, and work up into a lump.

If the butter is to be salted on the worker, sprinkle the finest and driest salt over the granular butter, ½oz. to the lb. for mild, and ¾oz. to the lb. for salt or potting butter.

Butter Making.

After salting place the butter in a cold but sweet apartment or cooler for six to twelve hours before making up.

For packing use prepared butter paper or cloth; never leaves of any kind.

Never pack butter when soft.

The cream may be salted if there is no objection to the buttermilk being spoiled—most of the salt going into it.

Miss Jacobs, the Blythwood head dairymaid, who has taken many prizes, says that as a rule she obtains one pound of butter from a quart of cream; but then Jerseys give very rich milk.

A champion prize of £25 was offered by the English Jersey Cattle Society for the cow of any breed yielding the largest quantity of butter in proportion to her live weight. Graceful Maid, in the competition, yielded 2lb. 3oz. of butter in twenty-four hours, her live weight being 834lb. This gentle eyed, pretty, fawn-coloured animal calmly rubbed her nose into our hands, apparently not in the least conceited after her wonderful performance.

Sir James Blyth warmly declares that it may cost 5 per cent. extra to make really good butter, but that the producer can demand 50 per cent. more for it when made. Not a bad rate of interest!

I now proceed to give some particulars concerning what has lately been done in England and Ireland to establish co-operation, prefacing my statistics with a few weighty words from Sir James Blyth:

"The industry of dairying must, from the nature of things, be intimately associated with the well-being of every nation. Our object is to give information, encouragement, and help to the agriculturists of the United Kingdom. The power of our masses to consume is always increasing. It is our desire to stimulate the home production of articles of commanding excellence. Unfortunately, the ever-increasing demands of our urban populations is being met in far too large a proportion by foreign produce. Without the most careful and precise application of the best methods of manufacture, preservation, and distribution, we cannot hope to hold our own. New sources of supply are pouring their resources upon our shores in ever-increasing volume. Relatively to the nations now sending us their dairy produce, we have fallen decidedly behind. This relative retrogression is, too, of greater injury to our farmers than it ever was before. If superior quality were of importance when distances, measured by time of transit were great, how much more necessary is it for us to stand first in quality in the home market, when time, distance, and cheapness are in favour of the foreigner! . . . It is too often said that nowadays quality does not pay. By intelligence, energy, and perseverance, I maintain that it can be made to pay. Speaking as a business man of a business matter, I well know that the public are eager for genuineness and excellence in every article they consume. If sure of good quality in the home product, they prefer it to the foreign article, and will pay more money for it. Let the British farmer, therefore, whether individually or by association in companies, dairy societies or creameries, seek to improve and maintain the quality of his goods, so that his name or brand may be a guarantee of genuineness and uniform excellence. I look forward to the time when dairies of the most perfect construction and fitting-up will be part of every British homestead. My own dairy is, as you know, but a toy as regards that practical point of view—profit. Side by side with it, I regret that I have not had one built upon strictly commercial lines. Such a building can be erected, combining all the conditions of a thoroughly effective dairy, at a cost which would not add more than a farthing per pound to the cost of the butter produced by it. . . . In travelling over the world one cannot but perceive with pride that British goods of almost every description are preferred because of their superior quality. In fact, they become for this reason absolutely indispensable to the wealthy classes of foreign countries. Yet we find the British farmer, although in this article of butter he enjoys certain advantages of contiguity, soil and climate, distanced by his foreign competitors, simply because they pay more attention to small details of manufacture. Amid the darkness of the agricultural outlook some rays of light are visible, to cheer followers of this particular branch of dairying industry."

Butter Making.

There is a great demand for plans of cheap and practical dairy buildings, and Sir James Blyth has offered three prizes (each £100), to be awarded by the Council of the British Dairy Farmers' Association for each of the following :

1. Drawings, plans, or designs.
2. Models of a permanent dairy—size being limited to a square of six or eight feet.
3. A portable dairy on wheels which can be moved by a horse to any part of the farm like a gamekeeper's hut.

The result promises to be of the greatest value to farmers. What is required is an easily constructed building combining the indispensible requisites :

1. Equable temperature.
2. Perfect ventilation.
3. Good drainage.
4. Modern sanitation.
5. Every facility for expeditious working.
6. Cleanliness.
7. Durability.
8. Cheapness in construction—this point being of primary importance.

Several philanthropic folk have started butter factories as a means of helping their farmers and tenants, and, on the whole, their generosity has met with success.

In Kerry, Mr. George R. Browne inaugurated a creamery to help the farmers and his own tenantry, and to-day that one creamery has fourteen offshoots in different parts of the county.

Mr. Alexander Henderson has a large dairy at Buscot Park, Faringdon, also started to help the tenantry, where such excellent butter is sold at 1s. 4d. a pound all the year round, and sent out properly stamped with its guarantee, that it finds a ready sale, and the dairy is now a paying concern. Mr. Henderson says : " This year our average summer price for milk is 4·76 per imperial gallon; 3·52 gallons of this makes one quart of cream, and one quart of cream makes 1·18lb. of butter ; therefore as nearly as possible three gallons of milk makes a pound of butter. The winter price for milk is about 1d. per imperial gallon more than in summer."

There are many such factories as the above scattered over the country, most of which have been successful, some, indeed, remarkably so, in spite of the uphill battle and opposition they have had to fight. But hundreds should be started, and it is with this object I give such figures as may prove useful.

The East Sussex County Council has a technical instruction committee, which has organised and looks after a travelling dairy school. Now this is a system that should be organised throughout the length and breadth of the land. If the County Councils can work in conjunction with Lord Winchilsea's scheme, which is to be started this autumn, and the County Councils will see that the technical teaching produces good butter, then his Lordship's company will open depôts to receive that butter, and dispose of it in the most advantageous markets. The practical and theoretical must work together. This travelling dairy school can be sent to any village or district that makes an application, and the caravan, if such we may call it, and its teacher will remain in one place for two weeks in order to provide a regular course of instruction lasting ten days. There is, of course, a stipulation as to the number of pupils—ten being sufficient, and fifteen the limit.

All particulars as to this organisation, which is doing so much good by personal instruction, can be procured from Edwin Young, Esq., Organising Secretary for Technical Education, County Hall, Lewes. But still the system seems to be so excellent that I feel compelled to give the conditions and the list of lectures.

EAST SUSSEX COUNTY COUNCIL.

TECHNICAL INSTRUCTION COMMITTEE.

Travelling Dairy Show.—Conditions to be observed by Local Committees.

Before any application for the school to visit any district can be entertained, a local committee and a local secretary must be appointed at each centre to be visited by the school, who would be responsible for making the necessary local arrangements.

The Local Committee must comply with the following conditions:

1. The Committee must guarantee a sufficient number of pupils to form a class (the minimum number being ten).

2. The Committee must undertake to provide, for the use of the dairy school, a suitable building, with a good supply of pure water easily accessible, preferably within the building. *Note.*—Towards the expenses of the hire of a suitable room, the Technical Instruction Committee will consider any application for an amount equal to, and in addition to, the fees received from the pupils, each application to be dealt with upon its merits.

3. The Local Committee must defray the cost of any printing and advertising necessary for making the school known in the district.

4. The charge for a term of ten days' instruction will be 2s. 6d. per pupil. These fees will be the property of the Local Committee. A moderate charge may be made to visitors wishing to inspect the work of the students and listen to the lectures.

5. The County Council will provide sufficient milk or cream for use in the dairy school. The butter made may be sold at the end of each day's instruction.

6. The County Council will provide the teacher, without any charge being made to the Local Committee, and will also provide all the appliances required for use in the school.

Edwin Young, *Organising Secretary.*

County Hall, Lewes, *March*, 1894.

EAST SUSSEX COUNTY COUNCIL.
Technical Instruction.
Travelling Dairy School, under the Management of Miss Mabel F. Maidment, Lecturer.

Syllabus.

First Day.—Lecture on dairying in general with a demonstration of butter-making for public and students.

Second Day.—Lecture on the composition of milk constituents—Milking—Different yields of milk from different breeds of cattle—The necessity of cleanliness in cowsheds—Weighing and Testing of milk—Demonstration of butter-making—Students churn and make butter under the direction of lecturer and assistant.

Third Day.—Lecture and demonstration of different systems of cream-raising—The ripening of cream—Students churn and make butter under the instruction of lecturer and assistant.

Fourth Day.—Lecture on churning, washing and working butter—Making up the butter and packing for market—Students churn and make butter under the instruction of lecturer or assistant.

Fifth Day.—Demonstration of butter-making—Students churn and make butter.

Sixth Day.—Demonstration of use of separator—Students churn and make butter under instruction of assistant.

Seventh Day.—Same as Fifth Day.

Eighth Day.—Same as Sixth Day.

Ninth Day.—Same as Fifth Day.

Tenth Day.—Examination for certificates in practical work under lecturer.

Butter Making.

A very good work is indeed being carried on both in East and West Sussex. Below is a syllabus of lessons or lectures given at each school on the consecutive days of the ten days' course of instruction at each centre; also names of centre; and an analysis of the status of the students who attended the schools in West Sussex:

DAIRY WORK.

	No. of Lessons.	Average Attendance.		No. of Lessons.	Average Attendance.
Arundel, Rustington	10	16	Barcombe	10	16
Horsham, Warnham	10	16	Burwash	10	15
,, Rudgwick	10	9	Heathfield	20	12
,, Slinfold	10	14	Hurstmonceax	10	16
,, Billinghurst	10	13	Hurstpierpoint	10	16
Petworth, Bignor and Sutton	10	14	Mayfield	10	12
,, Pulborough	10	10	Seaford	10	17
,, Wisborough Green	10	8	Ticehurst	20	10
,, Kirdford	10	13	Turner's Hill	10	18
Steyning, Storrington	10	8	Uckfield	10	16
,, Henfield	10	10	Whatlington	10	11
Worthing, Clapham	10	12			

12 centres; 120 lectures given; 11·3 average attendance.   11 centres; 130 lessons; 14·5 average attendance.

The full attendance possible at each class is 16.

Analysis of status of pupils in West Sussex:

Wives and daughters of farmers	49
Dairymaids	28
Domestic servants	15
School girls	8
Dairyman	1
Farm bailiffs	2
Farmers	3
Governess	1
No occupation	17

To show how much the farmers think of good teaching, it is worth stating that the late Lord Vernon started, in 1882, a creamery at Sudbury, Derby, for the purpose of giving practical instruction to those who cared to take the subject up. So highly was this appreciated, that the creamery increased enormously, and finally, about four years ago, had to be turned into a company. Mr. Algernon Fawkes, who supervises it, is one of the strongest advocates of co-operation.

After much practical use he is satisfied that artificial cream separation is by much the most satisfactory, not only for the cream, but as regards butter, which he declares will keep much longer and sweeter if the cream be taken from the milk by a separator than it would if allowed simply to rise as was the custom formerly. But, he adds, you must add uniformity to quality if you wish the butter to sell for anything like its real value ; and this seems to be the cry on all sides. *It is not only butter that is wanted, but uniformly good butter.*

As the want of uniformity is one of the greatest drawbacks to the success of dairying in this country, it seems only natural to suggest that the good butter should have a brand, a sort of hall-mark like the "gilt-edged butter" which fetches a dollar (4s.) a pound in New York, and is largely in demand. If our leading farmers and best creameries stamped all their butter as a guarantee of its quality, the public would gladly pay a little more a pound in order to feel certain that the article was first class. Wines, beers, &c., are labelled, why should not butter be ?

Butter Making.

There is a delightful little book called the "Dairyman's Year Book, 1895," edited by the Earl of Winchilsea, published at 30, Fleet-street, at a shilling, which gives many useful hints to dairy farmers, dealing with the management of the dairy, food for cattle, &c., besides hints such as " The best way to start a dairy farm ; How to stock one for £200," &c. Here is a quotation on

THE POINTS IN JUDGING BUTTER.

The following is Professor Sheldon's scale of points for judging butter on the basis of 100 for perfection :

Positive Qualities.	Negative Qualities.
Flavour.—Agreeable, clean, nutty, aromatic, sweet, pure, distinct, and full. 25	Strong, varied, tallowy, cheesy, stale, insipid, too stale, too fresh.
Keeping.—Inclined to slow changing, indicative of stability in retaining good qualities. 20	Early loss of good qualities and assumption of bad ones, indicating rapid change.
Solidity.—Stiffness of body, firmness, not easily melting or becoming soft. 10	Softness of body, unable to stand firm, easily melting or becoming soft.
Texture.—Compactness, closenesss of grain, breaking into a distinct fracture like cast iron ; fat globules unbroken and perfect, sticking little to trier. 15	Openness of grain, salvey, greasy, sticking to trier or knife in cutting, pasty, not breaking with distinct fracture.
Colour.—Pleasing, natural, not appearing artificial or even too bright. 15	Excessively deep or pale, appearing artificial, dull, uneven.
Make.—Includes all not included under the other points, as cleanliness, perfect separation of buttermilk, proper handling of milk and butter, as churning, salting, and skilful packing, &c. 15	Uncleanliness, imperfect churning, or at bad temperature, uneven working, salting, or messy handling, packing, or moulding, &c.

The following extract from a report on the Glynde Dairy is interesting because it shows that success may be achieved despite many disadvantages :

> The business is worked as a limited company independent of the farm, and all accounts are kept strictly separate. The capacity of the existing plant is sufficient to deal with 3000 gallons per day, but the present supply ranges only from 750 gallons in winter to 1500 in summer—an average of about 1125 gallons. Most of this is delivered to the factory direct, but a small quantity comes by rail, which entails a considerable extra expense. Two engines (15 and 5 horse power) are employed which pump water for the village, and thus increase the cost of plant very considerably, the whole of which is valued at £750, exclusive of building. A very liberal staff is kept up, consisting of a manager and two clerks, five men and lads, and two dairymaids.
>
> The chief object is butter making, though some cream cheese is made. The price of butter is 1s. 4d. to 1s. 6d. per pound, and never less than 1s. 4d.; and that of cream cheese is 4½d. per 3oz. cheese wholesale. There is no retail trade whatever. Much cream is sold at 2s. to 2s. 6d. per quart. The principal customers for these articles are retail grocers in London, Brighton, &c. The separated milk is sold wholesale at 2½d. per gallon delivered.
>
> The prices paid for milk vary according to the quality and time of year, but the average is within a fraction of 7½d. per gallon for the whole year, which is considered very satisfactory by the farmers. The net profit on the whole business is £5 per cent. per annum.

In Ireland great things have been and are being done. The Irish Agricultural Organisation Society, Limited, was formed by the Hon. Horace Plunkett, M.P., in 1889 with fifty members, and the following table shows its rapid increase of membership:

1891	850 members.
1892	1050 ,,
1893	1250 ,,
1894	1650 ,,
1895	3800 ,,

Butter Making.

These figures are startling, and prove how a little scheme in six or seven years has developed into an enormous society, and, as we all know it is the beginning of everything that is difficult, we can now realise by what leaps and bounds this society will go ahead. The sales of the Co-operative Agency Society, which is an offshoot, in 1893 were £45,575, in 1894, £64,858.

To give some slight idea of the Co-operative Agency's working and labours, I append some portions of a speech made by the Hon. Horace Plunkett, Chairman of the Association, in Dublin on May 8th, 1895:

> When a large number of Irishmen who differ widely upon questions of both political and religious controversy agree to form an association and to work together for what they believe to be the welfare of the agricultural classes, and when they support their action, not only by sympathy, counsel, and advice, but also by liberal subscriptions, they are assured of being given a hearing by their fellow countrymen. But, in order that they may be successful, something more than a hearing is necessary. Their proposals must be thoroughly understood, and they must be accepted and acted upon by those for whose benefit they are made. For our Society does not believe that it can, with advantage to the country, undertake any part of the farmer's business. But it is confident that it can, with the knowledge at its disposal, gleaned chiefly from other countries, show the farmer how to improve every branch of his business.

> Our Society starts with the belief that Irish farmers are capable of combining and working together just as well as those engaged in other industries at home, or as farmers in other countries. Indeed, we go so far as to believe that if we persevere in our work we shall soon see those engaged in every branch of agriculture successfully organised on the best foreign models. To this

end we are urging farmers to form societies in parishes or other suitable districts all over Ireland for the more profitable carrying on of the farming business in each such district.

But it may here be mentioned that quite apart from what we may call the trading advantages of farming organisation, an immense educational advantage will be experienced when farmers combine. Without any increase in expense or labour, all kinds of farming can be carried on much more profitably when the farmer is kept fully informed as to the best methods of tillage, and furnished with the best advice as to breeding, rearing, and fattening of live stock. Such information is easily spread and exchanged among farmers who meet together and work together in societies for mutual benefit. It never spreads among farmers who live in jealous exclusion from the society of their neighbours. Besides, the societies, especially when they are federated together as will be next explained, form an easy channel for the dissemination of useful information by leaflets, pamphlets, &c. *The Irish Homestead* newspaper has been started under the auspices of the Irish Agricultural Organisation Society, and has already done much to facilitate organisation and spread knowledge. Lectures, shows, ploughing and dairying competitions, and many other useful means of advising and informing farmers can be managed, when once we have an organisation to get up and carry through these useful aids to knowledge.

Now, while we hold that there is no district in Ireland where the farmers cannot do much better for themselves by combining with their neighbours for various purposes, this is only the first step in organisation. We well know that there are certain large questions which can only be properly dealt with by a central body truly representing the Irish farmers at large. Such questions are the carriage of Irish produce both in Ireland, across the Channel, and in England; the regulations regarding disease and infection; that part of national education which instructs both children and grown people in the elementary and more advanced theory and practice of agriculture and so forth. But we believe that such a body, to be fairly representative and thoroughly competent, can only be formed in one way, namely by delegates sent up from the farming societies throughout Ireland. This plan will be energetically pressed forward. As soon as a sufficient number of districts have been organised we shall ask the new societies to send delegates to a conference to discuss the constitution of this central body, and to take steps to organise it. The first conference will be the crowning work of the Irish Agricultural Organisation Society. In five years at the longest—and we hope much before—our society will no longer be required. In its place, if our scheme works out,. the farmers will have their own body—their Central Chamber of Agriculture, perhaps, they will call it—and through this body they will be able, not only to safeguard the general agricultural industry of Ireland, but also to attend to the organisation of fresh societies, in districts—just as we, who are setting the ball rolling, are doing, until the farmers are ready to take the matter into their own hands.

In conclusion we ask those who are not already acquainted with this scheme to think it out for themselves. We know well we are asking them to take a deal of trouble ; but we cannot see any other road to prosperity. A terrible depression hangs over British and Irish agriculture. The causes of this depression cannot all be dealt with. But at any rate we can join hands and hearts and heads together, and make the most of things as they are. We can improve our work, we can get better terms with those who handle our produce, and can get more money for productive purposes. One advantage we have—nearness to the best market in the world. We must get a better place in that market for our produce. Considering how far more important our agriculture is than all our other industries put together, surely an effort for its improvement is worth making.

The Secretary of the Association, and a very earnest worker in its behalf, is Mr. R. A. Anderson, whose own words are so very much better than any I could give that by his kind permission I reproduce the following :

CO-OPERATIVE DAIRYING : WHY FARMERS SHOULD SUPPORT IT.

By R. A. ANDERSON, *Secretary of the Association.*

Ireland was once the greatest butter-producing country in the world. Irish butter was considered superior to any other, and everywhere it obtained the highest price. This was only a few years ago, yet in that short period it has had to give place to butter from Denmark, from Sweden, from France, from Canada, and even from far-away Australia and New Zealand.

Why is this? Our butter is as good as ever it was—perhaps better. But England, which pays every year £12,000,000 for this foreign butter, says that it is better than ours, and it is ready to pay to these other countries a higher price than to us, *because they give it the kind of butter it wants.* England must have butter of exactly the same excellent quality every day in the week; *it must be uniform*—that is to say, it must be of the same colour, the same degree of saltness, and the same flavour. This is what the other countries supply, and this is why their butter fetches a higher price than ours. Theirs is excellent, uniform and reliable. Ours may be excellent in our opinion, but we cannot persuade the English buyer that it is, for it is neither uniform nor reliable.

Now, how have the dairy farmers of these countries managed to beat us at our own business—a business we have been brought up to, and on which so many of us depend for our living? This is how they did it.

They found out what the English market—the greatest market in the world—required, *and they combined together to produce butter which would please the Englishman, butter at once excellent, uniform, and reliable.* Then they combined together to sell their product in the English market without the intervention of unnecessary middle-men.

We, on the other hand, said to ourselves, "Our butter is good enough for us, therefore it is good enough for England."

So the English buyer has turned his back to Ireland, and has given the bulk of his trade to foreigners. It serves us right—but we have been punished enough, so let us try and see if we cannot make our *dairy cows pay as well or better than ever.*

The farmers in these countries which have beaten our butter back to the second or third place in the English market, have combined and have set up *creameries* of their own.

The rich farmer, with his fifty or hundred cows, joined with the poor man who had only one. This is called *co-operation.* Now we want Irish farmers to form societies and do likewise, wherever a district contains a sufficient number of cows to justify the erection of a creamery.

A creamery costs a good deal—perhaps £700 to £1000. This

Butter Making.

sum is subscribed in £1 shares, and it is easy to raise this large sum if everybody concerned takes as many shares as he can afford. Farmers generally take a share for every cow, but there is no fixed rule, the main object being to admit everyone who has a cow. These shares are paid up by four instalments of five shillings each, and interest is paid on them at the rate of five per cent. or a shilling in the pound. The first instalment is always paid in *cash*, so is generally the second, the other two may be paid by the farmer in *milk*. This will be explained further on.

The Co-operative Creamery—as it is called—is owned and managed entirely by the farmers who have taken shares. They are called "the members." They elect a committee to manage the business, the committee being formed of the best men in the society. Every member has a vote in the election of the committee, the man with one share having the same voting power as a man with two hundred. This committee appoints the manager, the dairymaid, and all the other hands employed in the creamery. It meets every month, or oftener, to examine the accounts, and to fix the prices for milk.

The farmers send in their milk, in the summer night and morning, in the spring and autumn once a day, and in the winter every alternate day. It is quickly run through the separators, which take out all the cream. When the milk comes in it is measured; then a sample is taken *to be tested*. All milk is not equally productive, so it would be unfair to pay the same price for poor as for rich milk. There is a testing machine now used in all the co-operative creameries which shows *exactly how much butter each supplier's milk will yield, aud he is paid accordingly*. This gives fair play all round, and the man who neglects or starves his cows, who keeps them till they are too old, or who puts water in his milk, or skims some of the cream off, is punished by getting a low price, while *the man who is honest*, and who treats his cows well, *gets the full value of his produce*.

In the co-operative creameries every milk supplier gets back his skim milk (or *separated milk* as it is called) free, also his share of buttermilk. For instance, a man supplying ten gallons of new milk gets back eight gallons of separated milk and about half a gallon of buttermilk. The separated milk is sweet and wholesome. Calves thrive well on it if they get enough and get it fresh. But it will well repay a farmer to give his calves some crushed flax seed (which can be bought wholesale at a moderate price by the creamery) after they have drunk their milk. Calves should be fed three times a day, at all events until they are four months old, and should be fed on new milk until they are three weeks or a month old. Farmers will not lose anything by so doing. Milk is cheap in the spring as compared with the autumn, and there will be a great gain in the increased value of the calf.

The Co-operative Creamery is your own—remember that. You can walk in and inspect the accounts at all reasonable times. You can see your milk measured and your sample tested. If you have a complaint you make it to a committee consisting of your own friends and neighbours, elected by yourself and the other members.

The accounts are *audited*—that is, examined and investigated—every six months by an official called a *public auditor*. A clear statement is made out by him, and is hung up in the creamery for the public to see.

There are 1,500 other Irish farmers, in six different counties, already joined in thirty-four co-operative creameries, the names of which are as follows :

    Co. CARLOW—Coolcullen, Milford.
    Co. CLARE—Kildysart, Labasheeda.
    Co. CORK—Doneraile, East Muskerry, Kilcorney, Lombardstown, Liscarroll, Lissarda, Skibbereen.
    Co. KILKENNY—Ballyhemon, Windgap.
    Co. LIMERICK—Altavilla, Ardagh, Ardpatrick, Athea, Ballyhahill, Bulgaden, Castlemahon, Clouncagh, Dromcollogher, Feenagh, Glenwilliam, Granagh, Glin, Grange, Newcastle West, Shanagolden.
    Co. TIPPERARY—Ballypatrick, Grange, Mockler, Glen of Aherlow, Mullinahone.

These have been organised with the help of the Co-operative Union of Great Britain and Ireland, which is now subscribing to the Irish Agricultural Organisation Society for the continuation of the work.

Besides these there are about ten new co-operative creameries preparing to go to work.

These creameries have established an *agency of their own* for the sale of their butter in England, Scotland, and Wales, and it is

Butter Making. 65

open to your creamery to join it. It is called the Irish Co-operative Agency Society, Limited, and its head office is in Limerick.

Your creamery can benefit you in many ways besides getting you a better return from your cows. It can collect your eggs and poultry, and sell them to the best advantage through the Irish Co-operative Agency Society. It can buy at wholesale prices, and in the best markets, your coal, your seeds, your feeding stuffs, your artificial manures, your farm implements and your machinery.

Farmers and others who wish to form dairy societies in their districts should communicate with the *Secretary*, *Irish Agricultural Organisation Society, Limited, 2, Stephen's-green, N., Dublin*, and speakers will be sent to explain the system, free of charge.

Issued 1st December, 1894.

That this society has met with valuable support is proved by the names on the formal prospectus, which the exigencies of space do not permit me to reproduce.

According to the returns of the co-operative dairies working in Ireland in April of the year 1894, the audited account of these societies shows the average yield of milk per cow per annum to be 435 gallons. "At the price for home-made butter last year—8*d*. per lb.—this quantity of milk would return the farmer (estimating three gallons to produce 1lb. of butter) £4 16*s*. 8*d*. If sent to a co-operative creamery the return to the supplier would have been 435 gallons at 3½*d*., viz., £6 6*s*. 10*d*. (3½*d*. being the average price paid in 1894), or a gain of £1 10*s*. 2*d*. per cow in favour of the creamery."

Another important item on their programme is the adoption of the Continental system of agricultural credit societies. Consequently it was decided to make an experiment in this direction at

F

Doneraile, co. Cork. It is under the management of a local committee and a secretary, and makes several small loans for productive purposes or in order to effect economy. But as these banking experiments are outside the purport of this paper, and enter more into the realms of finance than dairying, we cannot go further into the matter.

The Irish Agricultural Society last year held 315 meetings; the result of which was that no less than thirty-four new societies were organised and registered, while fifteen societies have begun to organise themselves. Like its English sister, the I.A.O.S. has its own journal, called the *Irish Homestead*, which is issued weekly at a shilling, and is full of valuable information, as well as a detailed account of the workings of the association.

When one sees the wonderful advantage of cooperation in dairying, it is a perfect marvel to an onlooker that the same principle is not applied to all agricultural necessities.

Before concluding this chapter I may add that, though Professor James Long has doubts as to whether butter making in factories will really pay in England, he is the strongest possible advocate for cheese being made on the farms, and sometimes even in factories. Indeed, he says that the many varieties of cheeses imported from abroad, such as Camembert, Brie, Gruyère, and Neuchatel, could be made equally well in this country; and speaks of the manufacture of Stilton, in which he is much interested, as being most profitable.

I was delighted to find that his daughters have

Butter Making. 67

taken up the subject of cheese making scientifically, and with the most satisfactory result.

In connection with this matter I would also remark that the Canadian Government, having lately realised the opening there is for cheese in the English market, has offered 2d. a pound, by the way of premium, on every pound of cheese that reaches 10d. in Great Britain—another proof that other people on all sides see what a welcome England vouchsafes to foreign produce, the more of which they throw at our heads, the more we seem willing to accept.

In America cows are fed largely on green maize, which is the cheapest thing that can possibly be grown. There is an erroneous impression that green maize cannot be grown in England, but I have met a man who has done so for eight years consecutively, and finds it less trouble and cheaper than anything else, and where he lives, in the south of England, takes two crops annually off the ground by sowing trifolium or green rye or vetches—all of which are ready for cutting in the spring: afterwards the land is ploughed and maize put in about the beginning of June.

CHAPTER III.

THE foregoing pages have striven to demonstrate three things :

1. That an enormous import of dairy produce is daily entering our ports—which import means, of course, a corresponding export of English gold ;
2. That this import will ere long double, treble, quadruple, unless prompt measures be taken to stop an invasion which must otherwise ruin this country ;
3. That co-operation is the only mode by which uniformity of quality can be maintained, and consequently a regular demand at a fair price secured; and would now crave permission to say a few words concerning the person who, in my opinion, can convert Great Britain and Ireland to the true commercial faith, and restore the pastoral glories of old to the Rose, Shamrock, and Thistle.

That person is Woman—it is She who can save her country—it is to Her I appeal.

When our butter was the best in the world, our pork excellent, our cream and milk good exceedingly, our fowls plump and tender, our eggs delicate and plentiful—who superintended the dairies, poultry yards, and styes? Woman.

In those old days it was not the farmer who attended to such matters—it was the farmer's wife or daughter. As a rule, the farmer permitted his wife to keep the profits accruing from dairy produce as her own perquisite. She gave her time either as worker or overseer, and received her fairly earned wage in return.

One evil day, however, all this was changed. Whether the Serpent—who is just as busy now as he was in Paradise—put it into the woman's head that she would like the wage without the work, or suggested to the man that there was no profit in paying for the keep of pigs, poultry, and cows if he received nothing in return save a few flitches of bacon, milk, eggs, and an occasional fowl for his household, history does not record—the only fact we know is "that things were put on a different footing," with the result dairy profits speedily became so small farmers practically ceased dairying.

It is women who ought to take it up again, in a less idyllic fashion perhaps, but one which conforms to the money-making spirit of the times.

The finest opportunity possible now presents itself for letting them prove what they can do—an opportunity which may never occur again for making their country rich, and its rural poor happy and prosperous.

Let them, then, be up and doing. Let them tell their husbands, brothers, sons the simple truth, that in dairy produce there lies a gold mine in which every man and woman may at once take shares to his and her ultimate great profit.

At the present time work is not deemed a disgrace—quite the contrary, indeed, since we appear daily more and more inclined to accept St. Paul's dictum, "If any would not work neither should he eat."

As regards the gentle-born, the tables have turned in a marvellous manner. A century ago the ladies of England had spindle waists and wore satin shoes, which forbade their taking part in outdoor exercise; their education was somewhat limited, literature a luxury, and consequently they lived much the same kind of life that the Eastern woman does to-day. They remained cooped up in their homes, dressed like pampered dolls, fed on the best of everything, lived a life of idleness, with the result that all hard work, mental and physical, was in the hands of the lower classes, while dainty ladies did nothing but smile upon their lords, or ply their needles in the finest stitchery.

Times changed, however, and went on changing till things arrived at the present pass, when land is well nigh valueless, agriculture almost at a standstill, and even "consols" and "railway dividends" are lower than formerly. The professional man's fee has not increased, while his sons and daughters require double—aye, treble—the amount spent on their education and requirements which was formerly the case.

What is the result? Well-born ladies and gentlemen, grand folk who a hundred years since would have thought it *infra dig.* and menial to employ their hands or their brains, are now glad to find occupation and remuneration in every possible way. Amongst the upper classes labour is no longer considered degrading. The men are only too glad to get "something to do," and the women, year by year, are striving more and more to earn an honest living by their pens, their paint brushes, their needle, district visiting, or hospital nursing.

Under these circumstances it seems strange that ladies living in the country, possessed of only small incomes, should not ere now have set assiduously to work to rear poultry, or grow fruit and vegetables, for which there is an endless demand in our large towns; but it is not yet too late. If they began on a moderate scale and learnt their experience as they went along, they would soon find an appreciable difference in their means. Instead of migrating to large towns, where the female labour market is already overstocked, let them remain in the country and devote themselves to any rural industry for which they chance to have a liking—bee-keeping, fruit or flower farming, poultry rearing, &c.

Our farmers and cottagers do not consider eggs worth troubling about, apparently, judging by their scarcity; but eggs can be made to pay, nevertheless, even when taken in hand by a busy woman, as the following statement, quoted from Mrs. J. H. Riddell, the well-known novelist, will show:

> There can be no doubt but that poultry, properly managed, return a remarkably good profit. If anyone care to start, say with six hens and a cock of the old barn-door breed, he can begin his experiment at a cost of certainly not more than £1 1s.
>
> At the expiration of a year his hens will have repaid the first outlay, kept themselves, and returned a trifle besides. They will also have produced fifty chickens (this is a low estimate), and he would therefore begin his second year with, say, from twenty to thirty laying hens, for which he has had to pay nothing, the sale of the remainder settling the cost of keep for the whole number.

So far, large poultry farms have not proved a success; the reason for which probably is that the profit on poultry will not pay for expensive plant in the shape of model houses, wire inclosures, drinking fountains, incubators, and such luxuries.

Fowls must have a run, whether in a good yard, by the roadside, or in a field, but that run need not be large, if it be divided so that one portion may be "taking a rest" while the fowls are eating worms, insects, &c., in the other.

The great mistake that people make is that they do not feed their poultry sufficiently well.

Hens require good and regular food; then they pay. They need change of diet also—oats, barley, cheap wheat, and chicken rice—and plenty of clean water. Young chickens eat nothing worth speaking of. Any amount of money may, of course, be wasted in the process of rearing, but the best plan is to give them rice, crumbs, &c., and leave them to their mothers, who will scrape for them and keep them warm.

We learn from an interesting book just written on chickens that in a certain part of Hampshire the inhabitants have started fowl rearing by division of labour. Hatching and rearing up to a certain point is done by the cottagers. As soon as the eggs are hatched, they peg the hen down by the roadside (that is, tether her among the wayside clover) beside a rough deal box, into which she can retreat in bad weather. The chickens, of course, are at liberty, and forage for seed, insects, and worms within a short radius of the mother. As very little attention is required, a number of broods can be reared in this way. Eventually the farmer buys them up for fattening purposes at prices varying from 9*d.* to 2*s.* a head. This experiment is paying in Hampshire. Let us hope it may soon spread throughout the length and breadth of the land.

While speaking on this subject, I venture to adduce

Butter Making.

an instance of much-occupied people who yet succeed in making farming pay.

About twenty-five years ago, two ladies—the Misses Metcalfe, of Highfield, Hendon—started a small farm of ten acres in order to supply in a measure their large household, which, being a school for girls, necessarily requires a large quantity of milk, cream, butter, and eggs weekly. According to Miss Metcalfe, their scheme paid very well, and more land was added; but, tempted by success, in 1882 they took a still larger farm, and went in for pedigree cattle and pigs, also started a large poultry yard with runs for about six special strains. The result proved unsatisfactory all round, the yield of milk was less, and the litters of pigs scanty. The loss on the fowls alone was about £60 a year, and, though year by year they hoped for better days, in 1889 the larger farm was given up. The stock is now mixed Jersey, Guernsey, and shorthorns, all well-bred animals, but not strictly pedigree. Gradually the results have improved, until last year showed a good balance on the right side.

To give some idea of this delightful little organisation, I got Miss Metcalfe to look up her dairy produce in the last year. Her books are so splendidly kept that she was able to give me the facts at once, and told me that with an average of ten cows in milk she received in the year:

> Milk, 31,845 quarts; cream, 88 quarts; butter, 1721lb. (1 quart of cream makes 1lb. 6oz. of butter); from an average of 150 hens, 7666 eggs.

The amount of land now in cultivation is about

forty acres. Twenty-three head of stock, old and young, are kept. The pigs have supplied this year ninety hams, while a goodly number of young stores have been sold. These, with food from the dairy and house, are kept at a very small expense, and the happy liberty of fowls of all sorts and conditions produces more and larger eggs than when confined in the stately grandeur of their special runs; also the chickens and ducks thrive better, and are much more easily fattened for table.

Another point is the extreme accuracy with which the accounts are kept. Butter, eggs, milk, and cream are credited week by week at the ordinary rate of dairy produce; while against this profit every item of expenditure is put, and finally deducted at the end of the year, so that the above record, which seems decidedly satisfactory and encouraging to other ladies, may be taken as absolutely correct.

This is only a little farm looked after by women, most of whose time is fully engaged elsewhere. Of course, they are most ably seconded by an excellent bailiff, who carries out their plans with untiring zeal. The fact, however, remains that the Misses Metcalfe make their farm pay.

Co-operation, if carried out to the extent proposed, will open a wide field of pleasant labour to gentlewomen as dairymaids. Having taken up the subject seriously, studied the question from both its practical and scientific side, and made themselves thoroughly competent—what position could be more delightful than to be the head of a dairy? Indeed, several ladies already occupy this position in the country, receiving from £30 to £80 a year, with free rent. The opportunity that presents itself for ladies in this department, as also in fruit growing, jam making, and bee keeping, all of which industries can be carried out by the individual without any extravagant outlay of capital, or superintended by the expert at a very useful wage, seems to offer a better opening than that everlasting cry: "I must do something, so I shall take a situation as governess. or else go on the stage"—occupations at the present moment overcrowded by girls and women who have had no education whatever to fit them for such posts.

It rests with woman, as I said before, to help agricultural England to raise up her head once again, and produce her own milk, butter, bacon, eggs, vegetables, flowers, and fruit. England is to-day the money-box of half Europe. For the future let her women distribute the money which at present goes to enrich foreigners amongst her own children.

The cry is now: "Get the labourer back to the soil."

The labourer will never leave it if cultivated women stay there also and give him employment, which might on dairy farms be found for him easily *all the year round*. Women could do no finer or more patriotic work than that I have indicated. She who prevents distress is a better sister of charity than even she who relieves it!

But others must be up and doing also. All this import of foreign dairy produce is a national calamity —a calamity increasing yearly by leaps and bounds, and yet our farmers actually turn away in despair instead of manfully fighting the battle and showing the capabilities of agricultural England, thousands —aye, millions—of whose sons might be employed if the farmer would but realise that the remedy for the present disastrous state of things is in his own hands.

Unfortunately, however, our people are not so thrifty as they might be; and while the foreign labourer's wife turns every bone or vegetable root to account, our working man's spouse throws them away as rubbish unfit for food. There is more waste from bad cooking and want of knowledge, in the cottage kitchen, than in the grand *cuisine* of the wealthy.

All the scraps flung aside as uneatable would help to keep the fowls and the pigs, but our poor folk have yet to learn that the best source of wealth is economy. The Thrift Society, at Finsbury Circus, has done much good, but it is not yet as much known or as much patronised as it should be.

While speaking of the National Thrift Society and its excellent work, I may mention a branch about to be opened which promises to be most serviceable. A gentleman proposes building an industrial home to be occupied by ten or twelve lads, whom he will house and maintain and train, under competent instructors, in the following healthful and useful occupations: Horticulture, fruit culture, vegetable growing, bee farming, poultry farming, jam making, carpentry, glasshouse management, rustic furniture manufacture, and other suitable industries.

Butter Making.

The cost is estimated at £25 per lad per year, while it is believed that at the end of the second year most of the boys would be able to earn their own living, besides being possessed of a useful and healthy trade.

Now this teaching is particularly valuable. Horace Greeley, speaking about civilising Red Indians, said: "Catch the young ones early and knock the old ones on the head." And if the young folk are brought up to respect the land, and taught how to make use of its gifts, every one of these well-taught lads will be a help to the agricultural question, which at the moment is of such vital importance.

In conclusion, I need only say if landlords would but accept the fact that they could do much for themselves and their tenants by erecting creameries, and working together for their mutual good; if tenants would but help the landlords by undertaking to sell them cream; if the small farmers would lay to heart the experience of Denmark in rearing pigs on skimmed milk and scraps so that nothing be lost; if the cottager would keep fowls and arrange to supply eggs to a collector, who should call twice a week; and if ladies would help all these good works forward as they alone can, then great things might be done, and Agricultural England soon be herself again. Without energy, enterprise, and co-operation, however, nothing will be accomplished.

Butter, bacon, and eggs may appear trifles; but are not homes marred and fortunes made by trifles; and is it not such trifles as these that have brought gold to the coffers of Denmark, and may yet keep many young English lads and maids at home, instead of being banished to the colonies in search of bread, as, alas! soon bids fair to be the case? If we cannot beat our neighbours, surely we are capable of imitating their excellent example before it is too late. If we go on as we are at present doing, our meadow lands will be turned into one huge advertisement, and our cows and calves will have disappeared in favour of pills and soap!

The matter seems worth considering.

www.ingramcontent.com/pod-product-compliance
Lightning Source LLC
Chambersburg PA
CBHW020323090426
42735CB00009B/1381